Faces of The Mohawk Valley

Brigitta Field
with Dr. Ronald Labuz

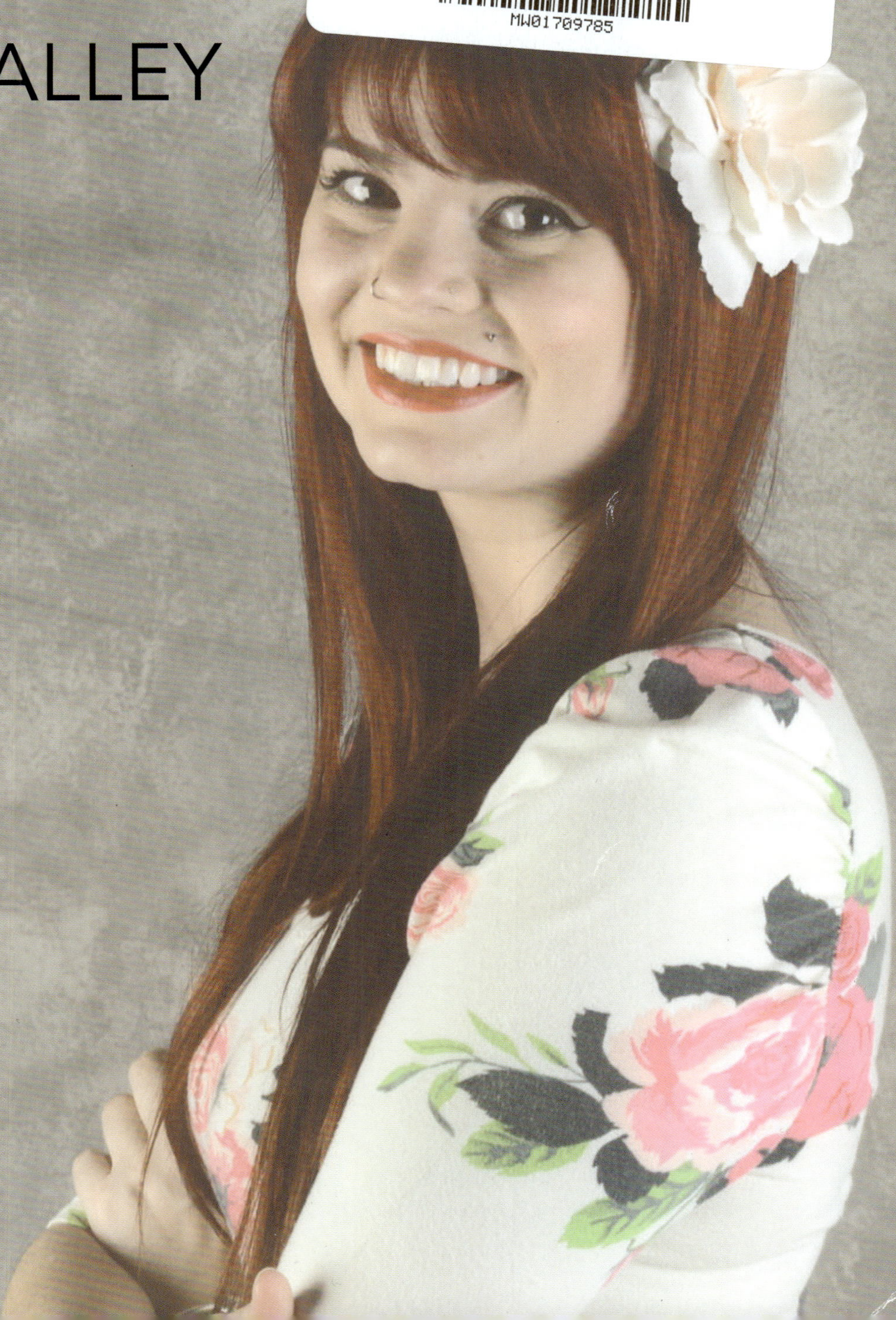

MVCC
MOHAWK VALLEY COMMUNITY COLLEGE

Artists and photographers are students from the Center for Arts and Humanities, Mohawk Valley Community College, 1101 Sherman Drive, Utica, New York 13501.

Designer: Ronald Labuz

Production Coordinator: Jim Vitale

Cover: Stephany Vargas, photograph by Aaron Deming
Back cover photographs: Todd Behrendt, Ross J. Deater, Kayla Emery, De'Anna Hopkinson and Frederick F. Zang

Proceeds from the sale of this book fund an annual scholarship awarded to a Mohawk Valley Community College student who has been assisted by the Mohawk Valley Resource Center for Refugees, 309 Genesee Street, Utica, New York 13501.

For information about this book or to donate to the scholarship program, contact:
MVCC Foundation, Office of Institutional Development
Mohawk Valley Community College
1101 Sherman Drive, Utica, New York 13501
frank.duross@mvcc.edu
315 792-5555

ISBN 978-0-9894562-0-3

10 9 8 7 6 5 4 3 2 1

Welcome

Dr. Randall J. VanWagoner
President

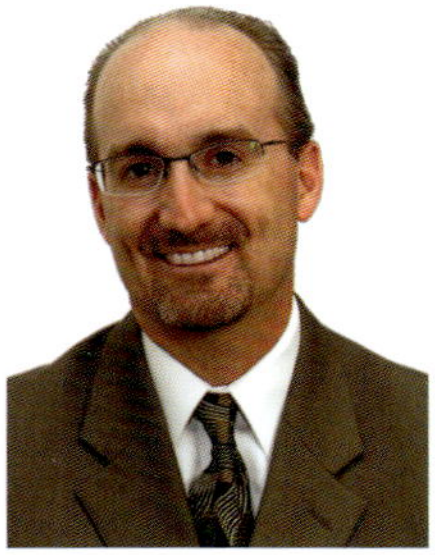

Welcome to *Faces of the Mohawk Valley*! The diversity of this region has been present for more than 200 years and this project seeks to provide a current tribute in modern form. From the early work of the immigrants who built the Erie Canal to those who followed in the mills and factories in the ensuing decades, the faces of the Mohawk Valley have been ever-changing. Subsequent generations of immigrant children have been joined by the recent wave of newcomers – refugees and immigrants alike – from all over the world. The region takes great pride in the welcoming spirit of the larger community that provides the rich diversity and adds to the quality of life here. *Faces of the Mohawk Valley* reminds all of us that our world is growing smaller every day, and the more we appreciate each other as individuals with our own individual stories, the better our world will be.

Faces of the Mohawk Valley

Dr. Maryrose Eannace
Vice President for Learning and Academic Affairs

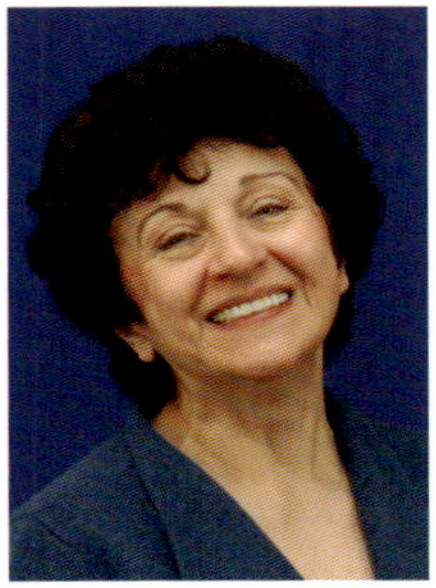

Faces of the Mohawk Valley began with our desire that all people who arrive on either of the Mohawk Valley Community College campuses will see something of themselves, their heritage, culture, history or family reflected through photography and other arts on our walls. We want people to feel at home here – to feel that they belong at our college. A small group of intrepid faculty and staff, students and neighbors brought in heirlooms and family photos that reflect their origins, while others agreed to pose for photographs and share their narratives. Professor Jerome LaLonde's photography classes took up the project that Professor Larry Migliori had helped to launch with School and Business Alliance intern Joseph Caldwell, and our walls began to evolve into a portrait of the heart of our community. Professor Sandra Engel edited narratives and Technical Assistant Todd Behrendt and his team arranged the community's mosaic of a project in the Information Technology Building and elsewhere. Within a year, *Faces of the Mohawk Valley* had become part of a national award-winning initiative.

The project further blossomed when Dean Lewis Kahler suggested the creation of this book. Professor Ronald Labuz invited School and Business Alliance intern Brigitta Field to help capture the celebration of community within these pages. I see this newest iteration of our project as an inspired invitation to come to the community's college to learn and share more of the richness and vibrancy of the Mohawk Valley. Welcome to these pages! Welcome to this community! And most welcome to this community's college…Mohawk Valley Community College – a learning community that celebrates our diversity!

Learning from Diversity

Brigitta Field
Intern, School and Business Alliance
Whitesboro High School, Marcy, New York

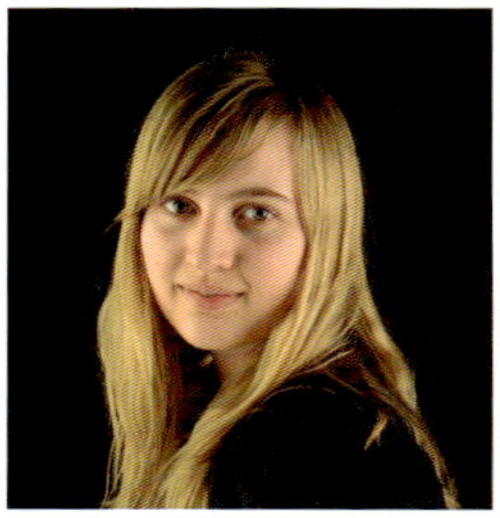

Before I became a part of it, *Faces of the Mohawk Valley* was an art exhibit filled with the photographs of students and community members portraying the diversity and individuality that exist in this area. When I was first given the opportunity to help commission new photographs for a book, I was thrilled. I immediately had an image in my head of what the finished project would look like – crisp colorful photographs with bold neat titles on the page, each showing the native country of the subject or her ancestors. Pages would travel methodically between continents until every country on the map was represented.

I began researching the many ethnicities in our Mohawk Valley. Krista Hartman of the Mohawk Valley Community College Library was instrumental in my success, and I'd like to thank her for the hours she spent showing me local history databases (that she developed herself) and helping me to find relevant information. Pavel Brutsky at the Mohawk Valley Resource Center for Refugees was also a huge help by offering me modern immigration statistics.

There is so much diversity living right alongside me in the Mohawk Valley, thousands of people with unique backgrounds, each with their distinct stories and histories. I soon realized that it is more than just ethnicity that makes a person who he or she is. As I met the people who were photographed for the book, "ethnicity" changed to "identity" and this book was transformed from being solely about cultural heritage to a book about individuals in the Mohawk Valley. I learned that I couldn't classify a person just by knowing where they were from and I began seeing their identity in the sometimes unexpected ways that each of us see ourselves.

If you flip a few pages and view the first photographs, you'll notice that there is no neat category identifying the face in each portrait. The book became more than I first thought. My initial vision for the book couldn't possibly portray the individuality and the wonderful diversity that exists here in the Mohawk Valley. Look in the back of the book to see how the people identify themselves, but first I hope you'll look through these pages and try to figure it out for yourself. You might be surprised by what you learn.

I'd like to thank Professor Ron Labuz and all of the super-talented artists and photographers who helped bring you this collection of art and life that exists right here in our community. I hope you discover for yourself the beautiful lessons found in these *Faces* and that you enjoy the book as much as we have.

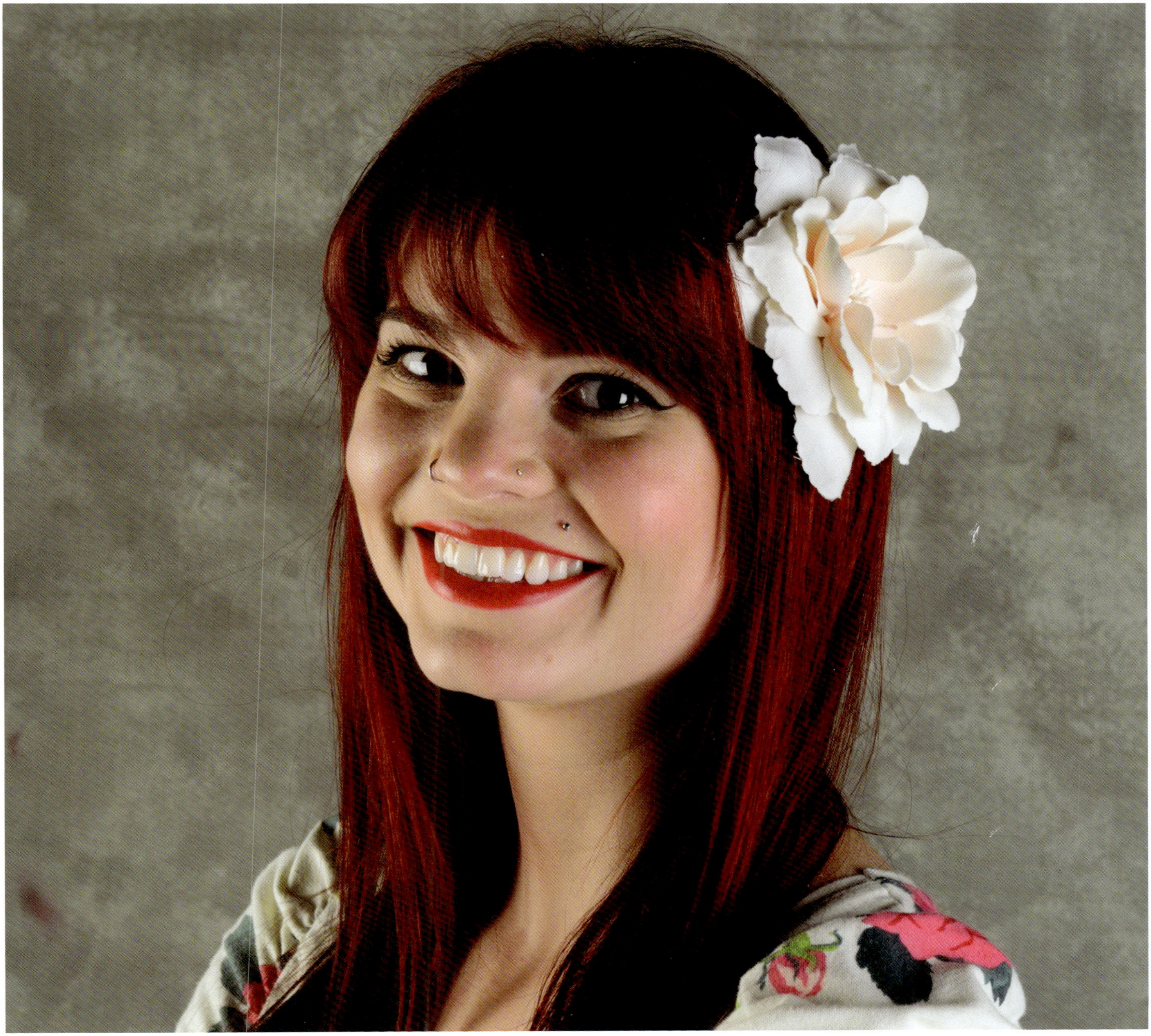

Alexis Valerie Nadeau
Photograph by David Lloyd

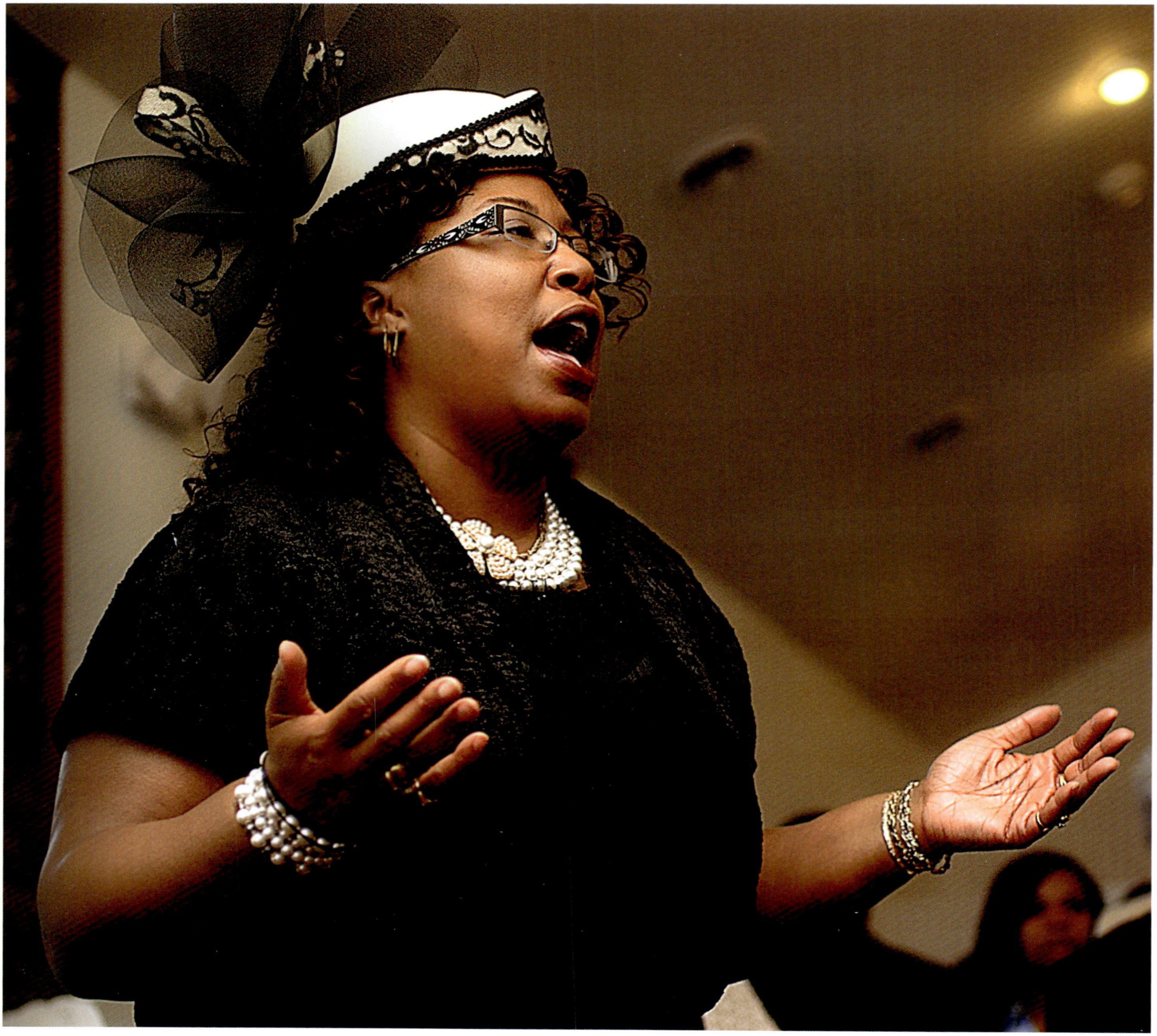

Evon Ervin
Photography by Michael LaPolla

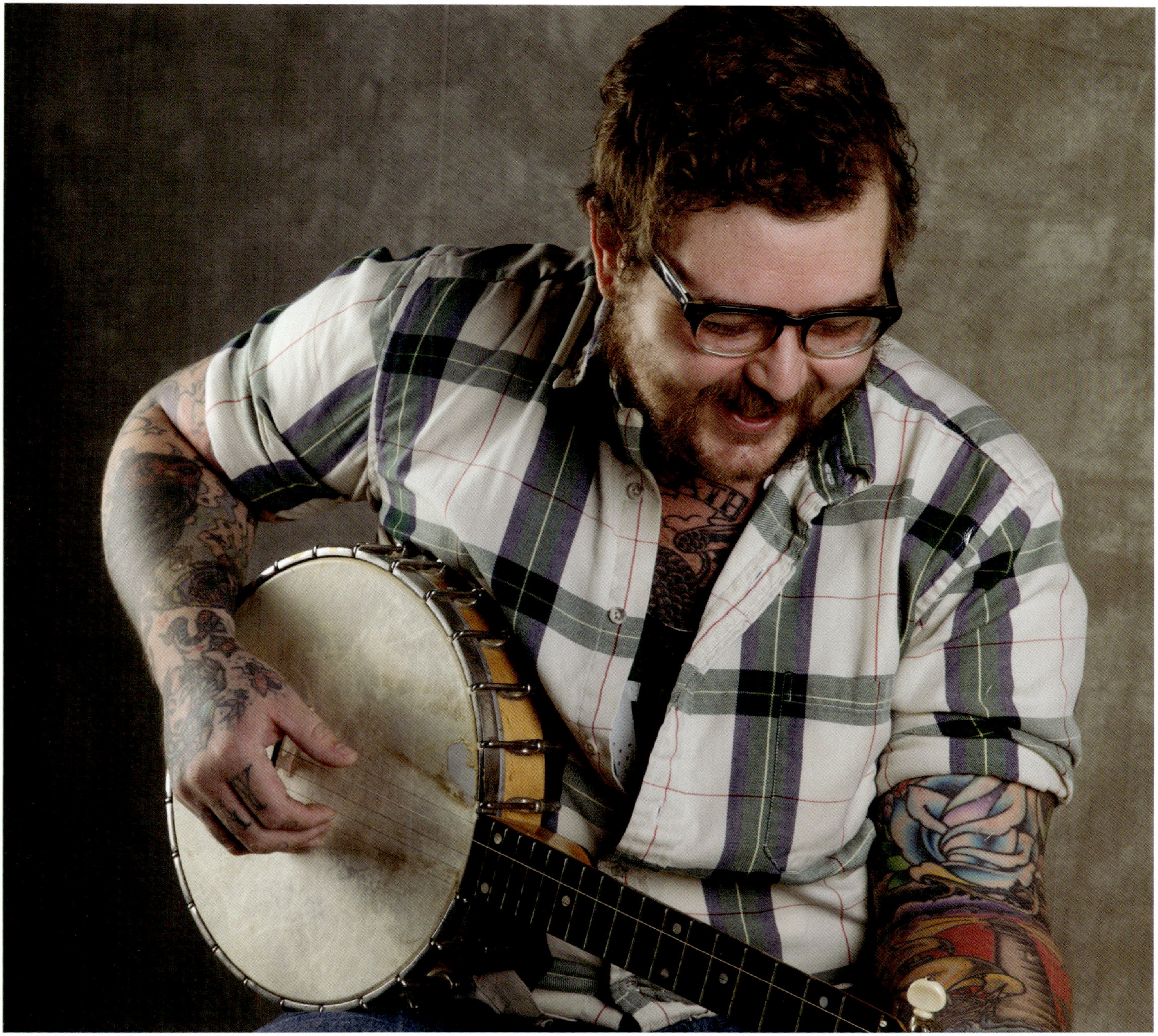

Dusty Elmer
Photograph by Anthony Zegarelli

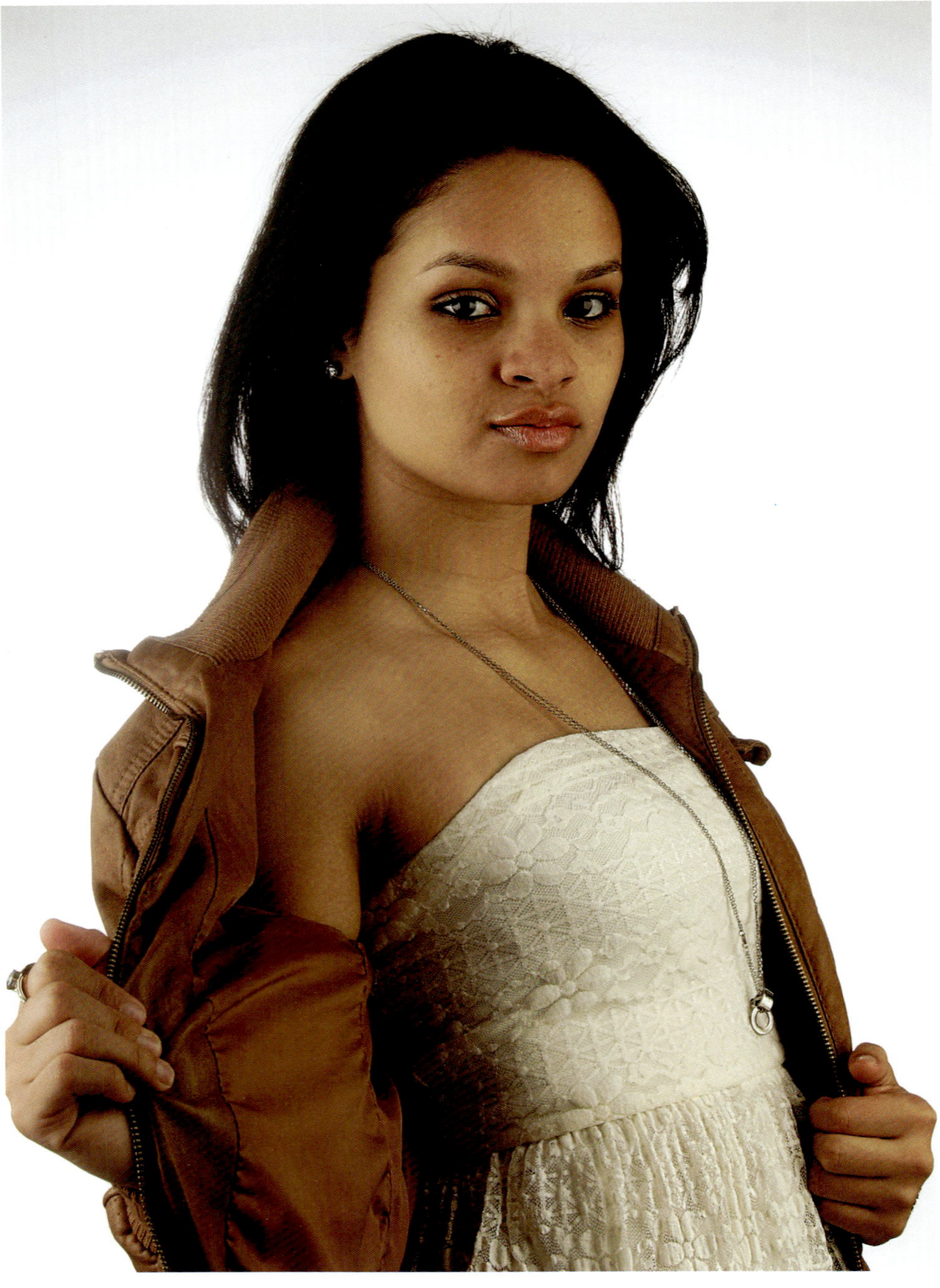

Indhira Grullon
Photograph by Kimmie Hilligas

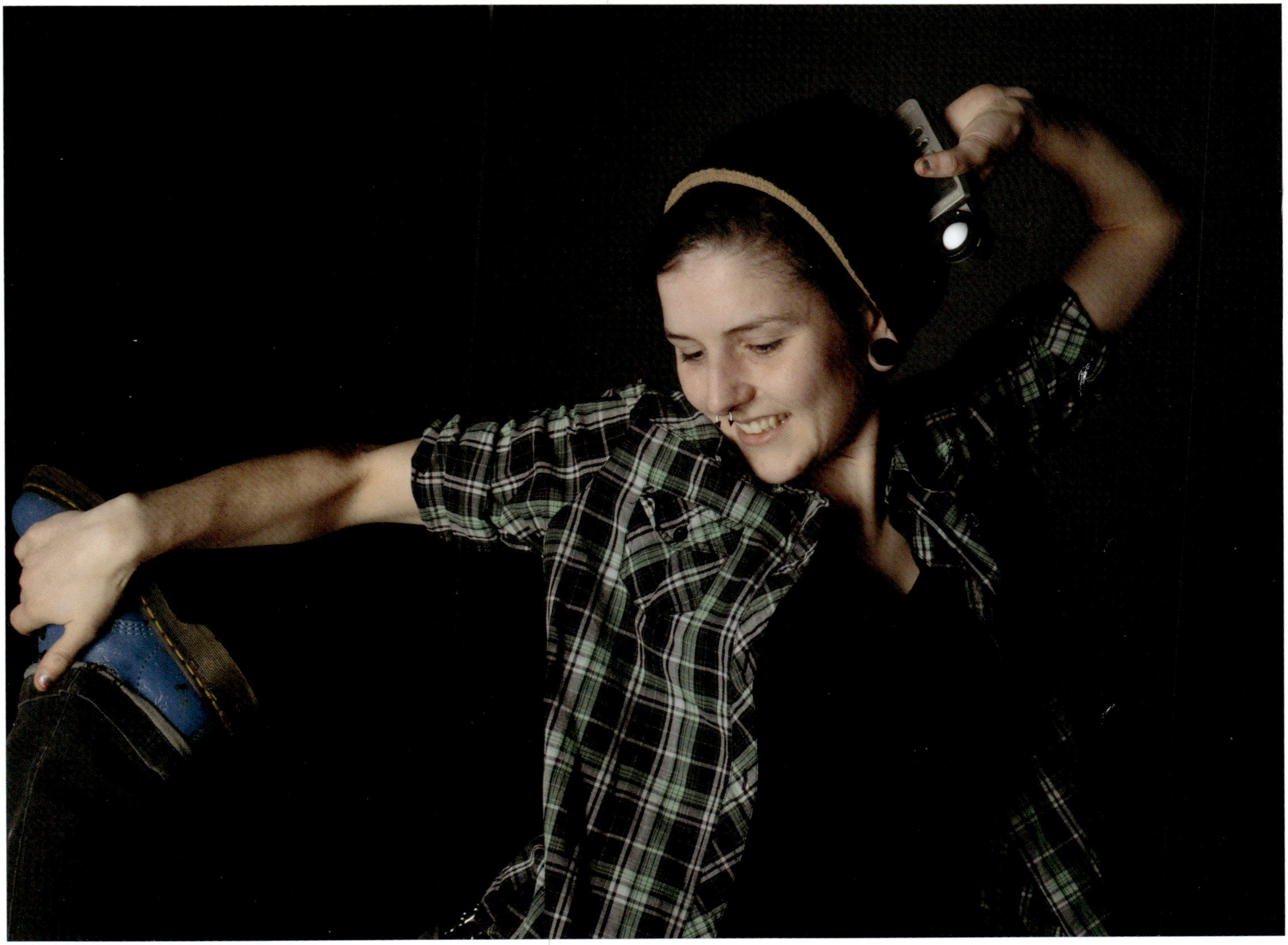

MacKenzi VanSlyke
Photograph by Eden Richardson

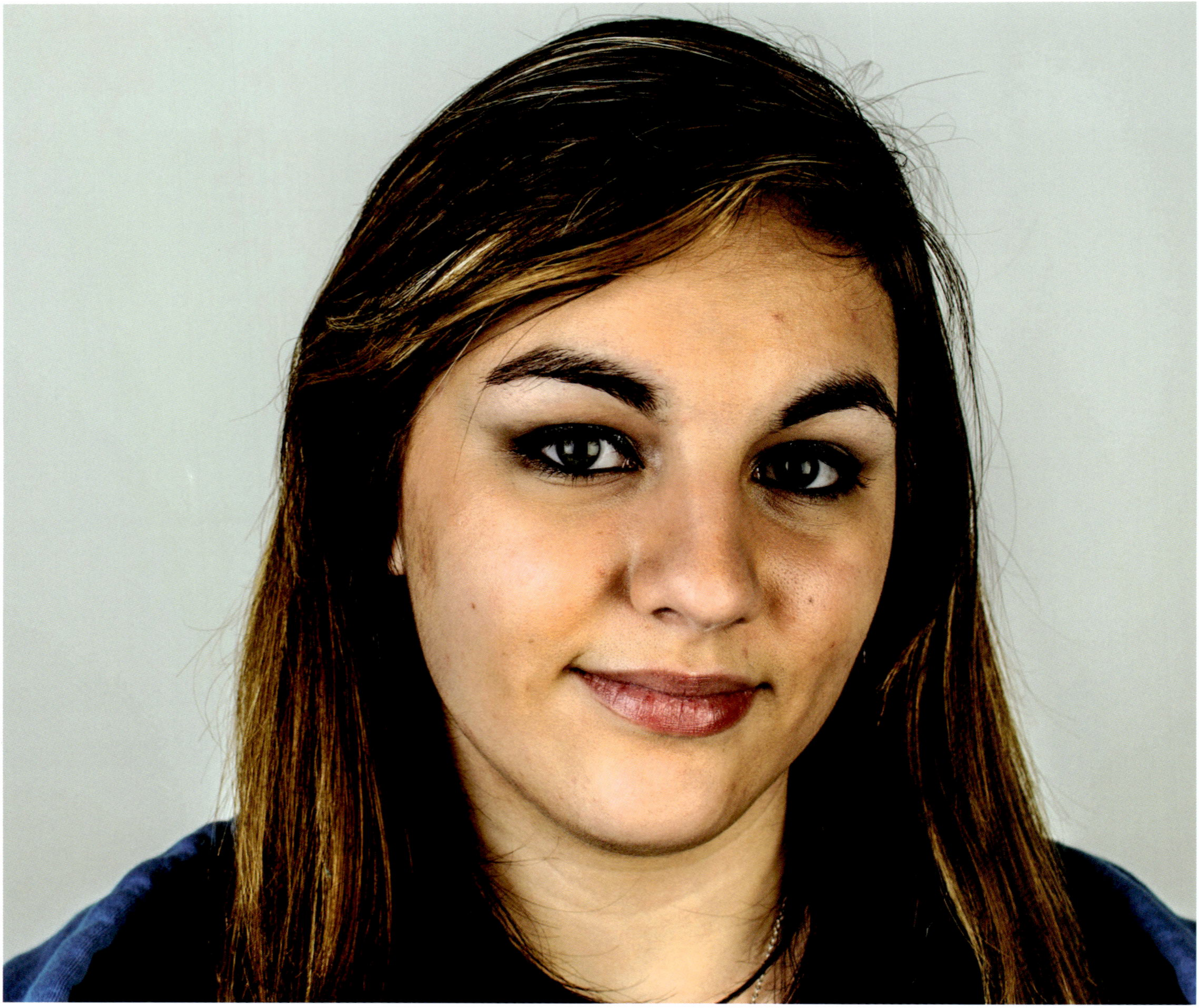

Rachel Ryther

Photograph by Eden Richardson

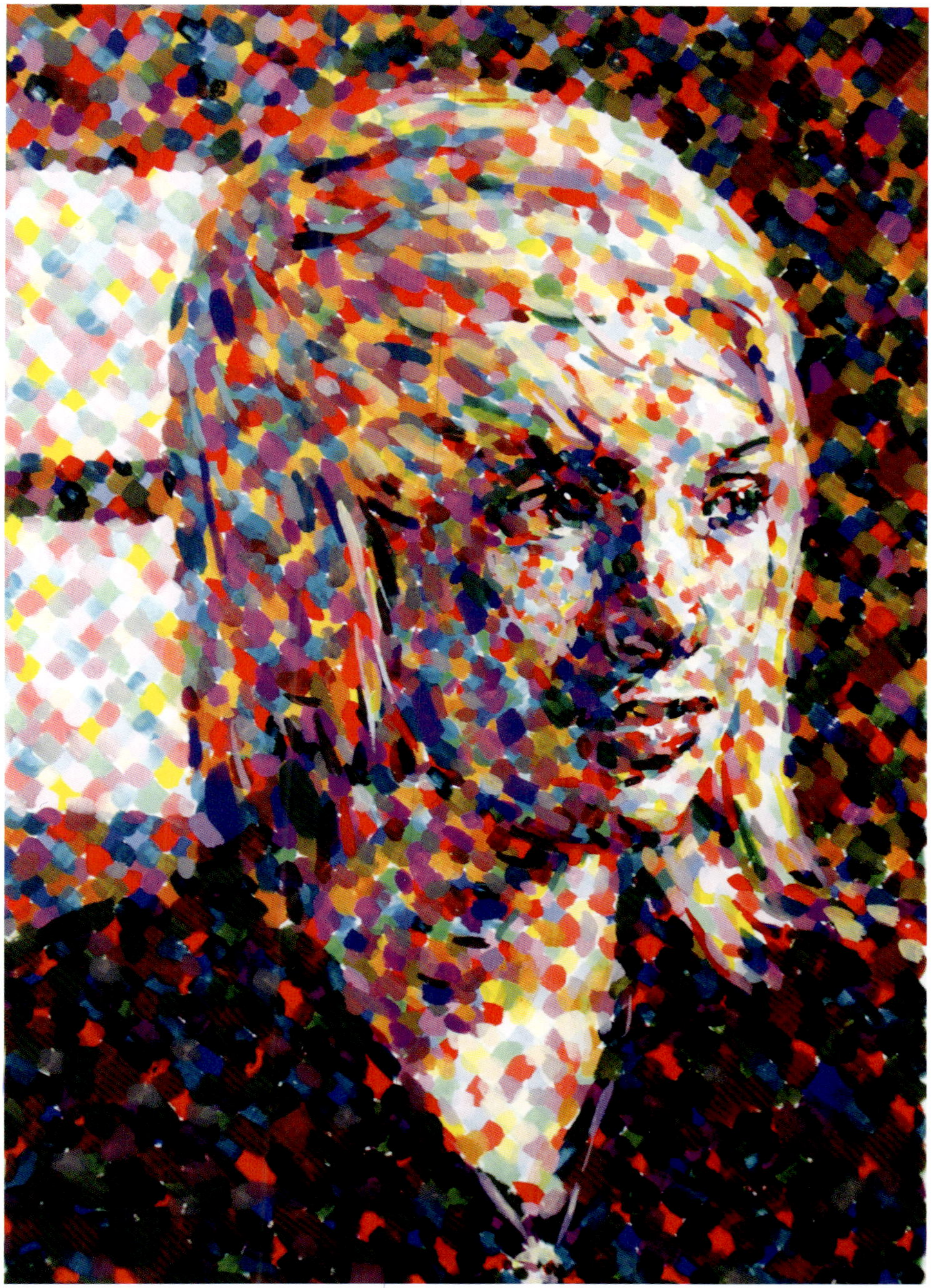

Victoria Storm Yaciuk
Painting by Jedediah Kimball

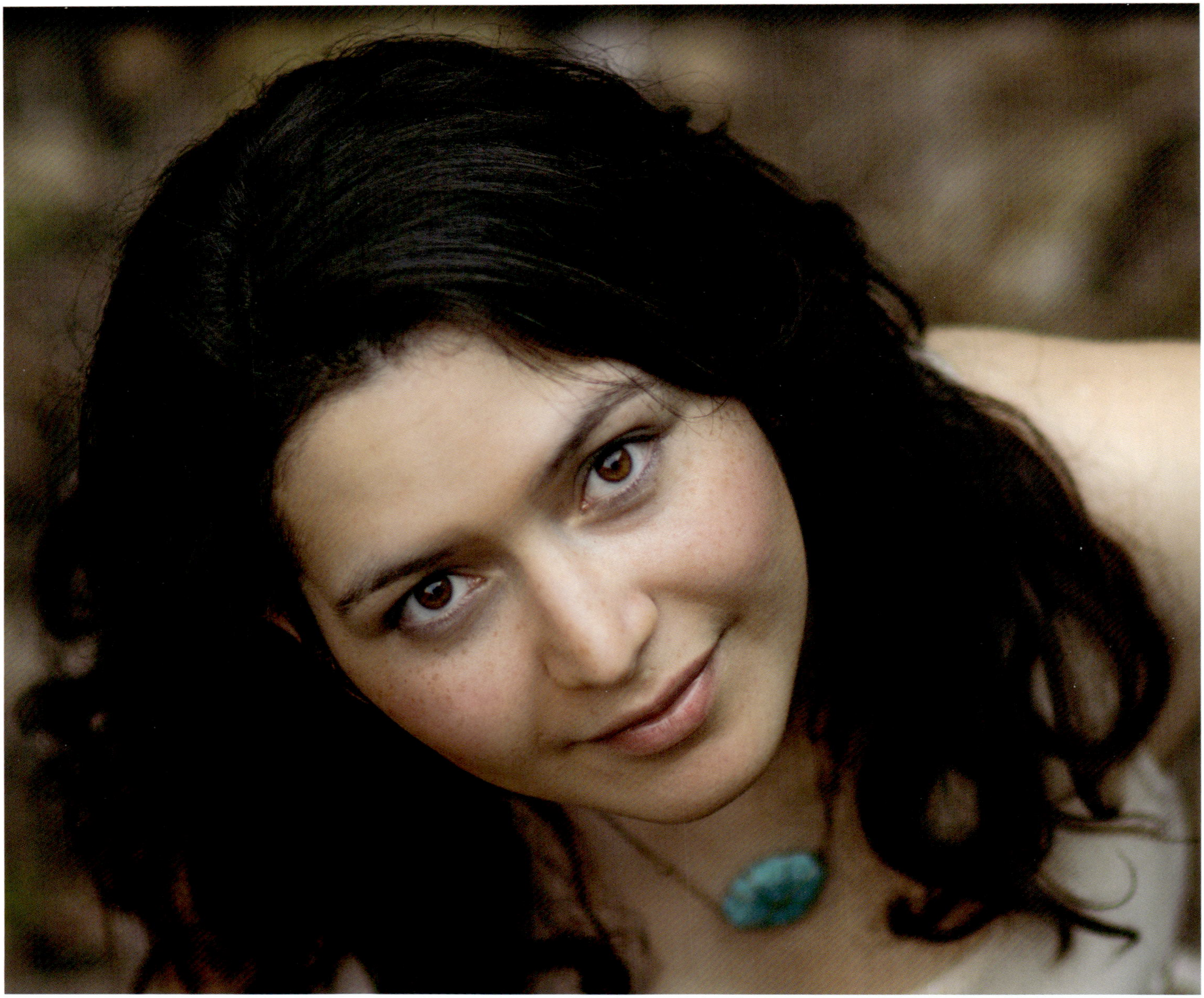

Diana Aguilar
Photograph by Ross J. Deater

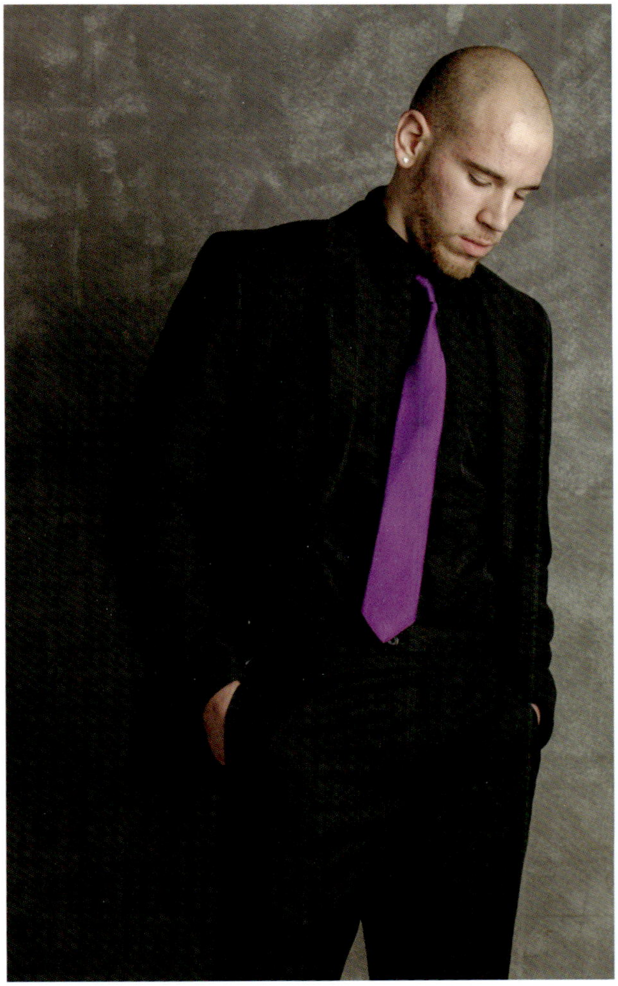

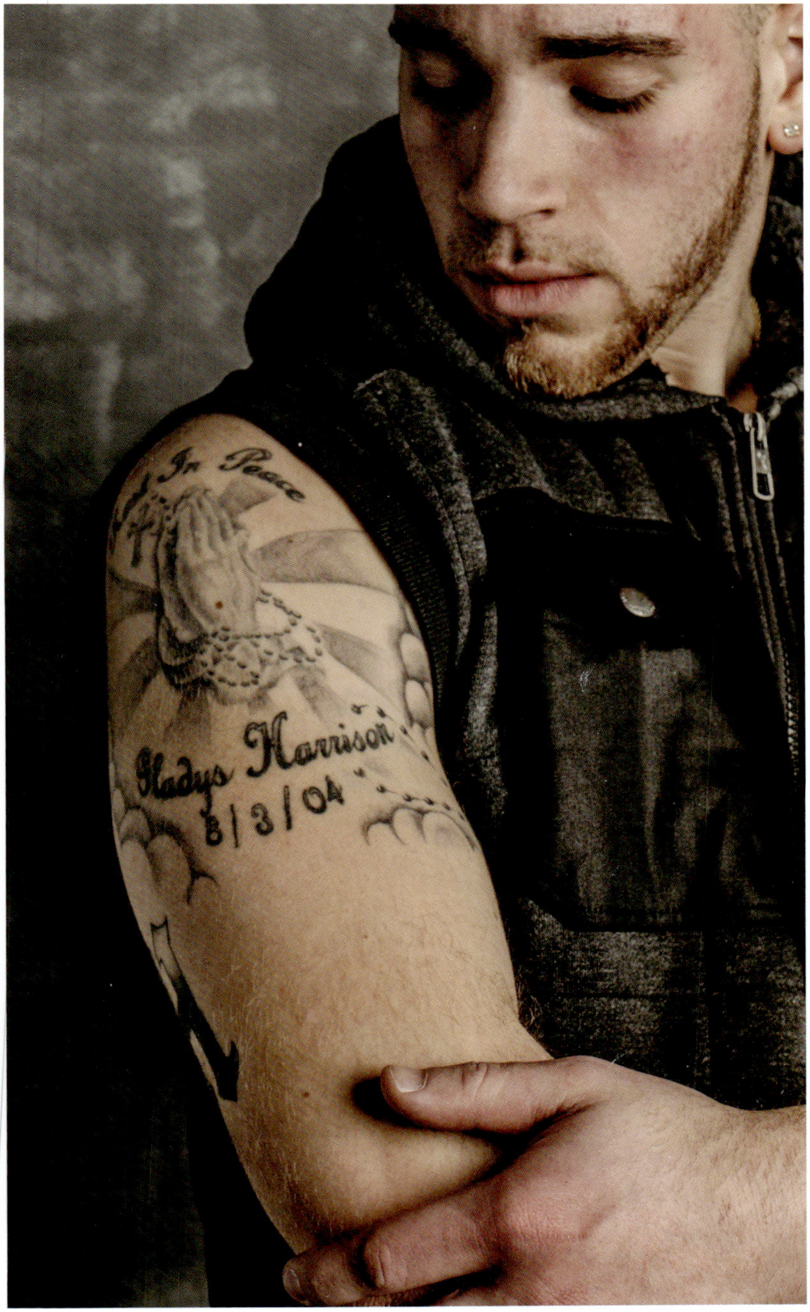

Joseph T. Harrison
Photographs by Kayla Emery

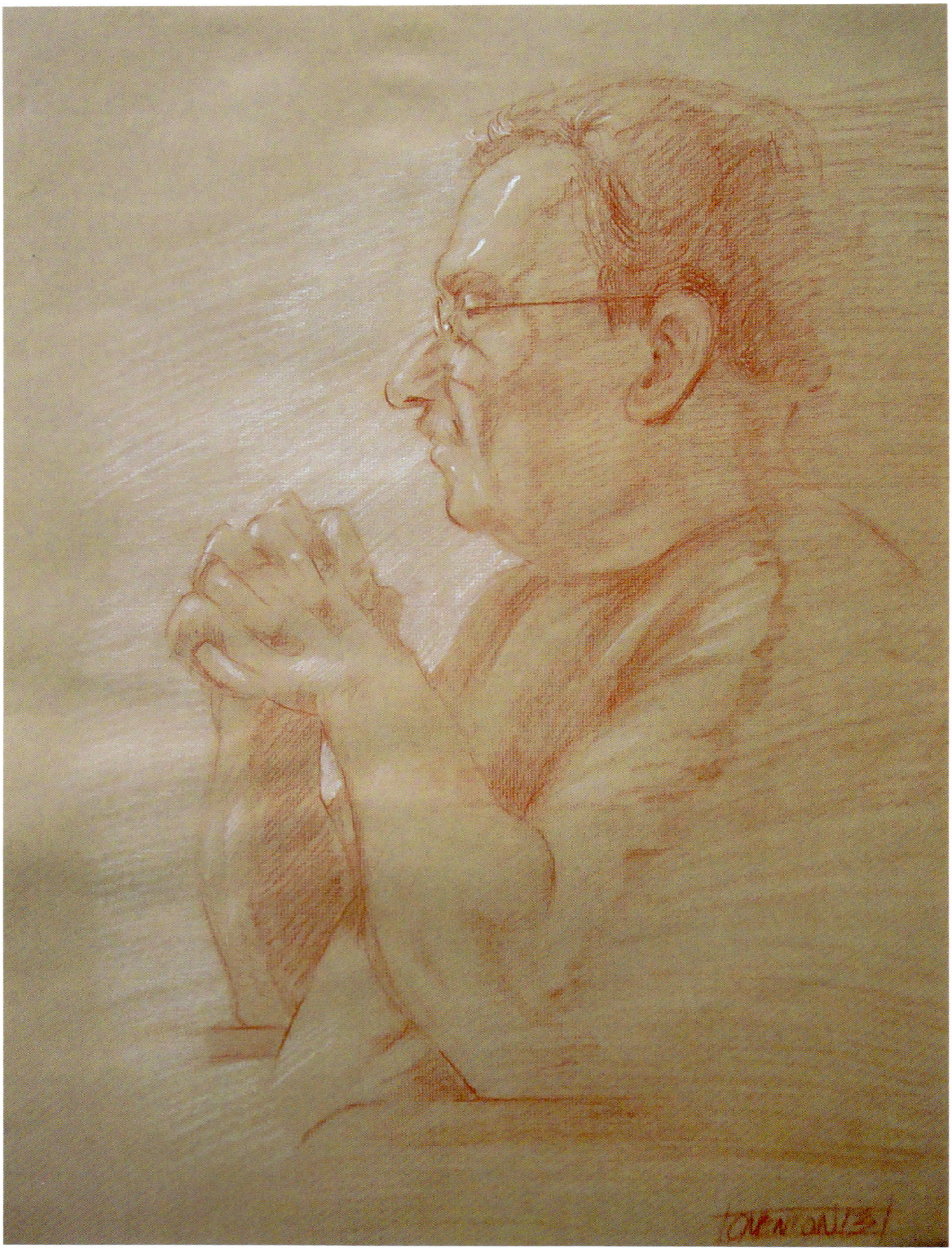

Steve Mazza
Drawing by Corey Newton

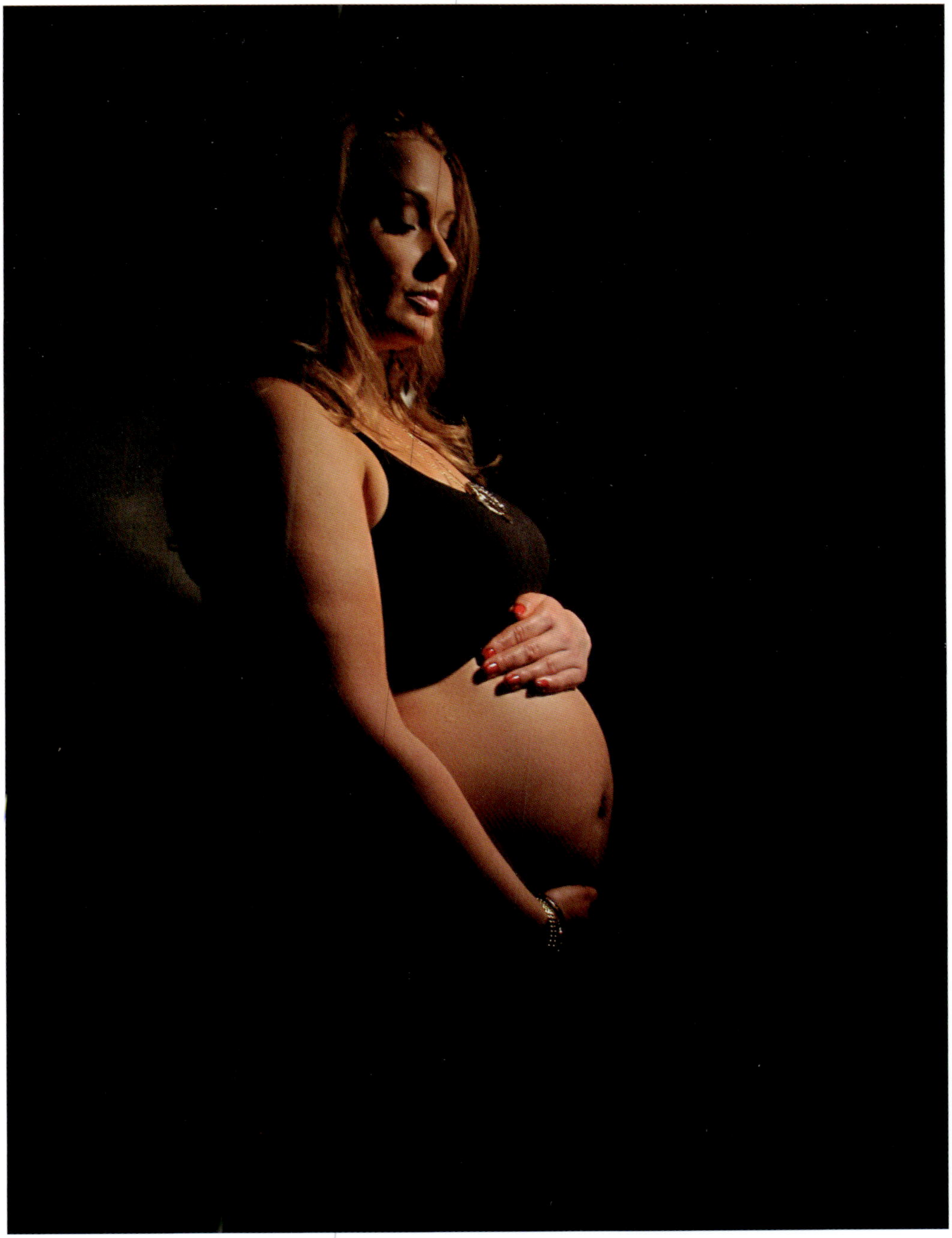

Nicole Stanley
Photograph by De'Anna Hopkinson

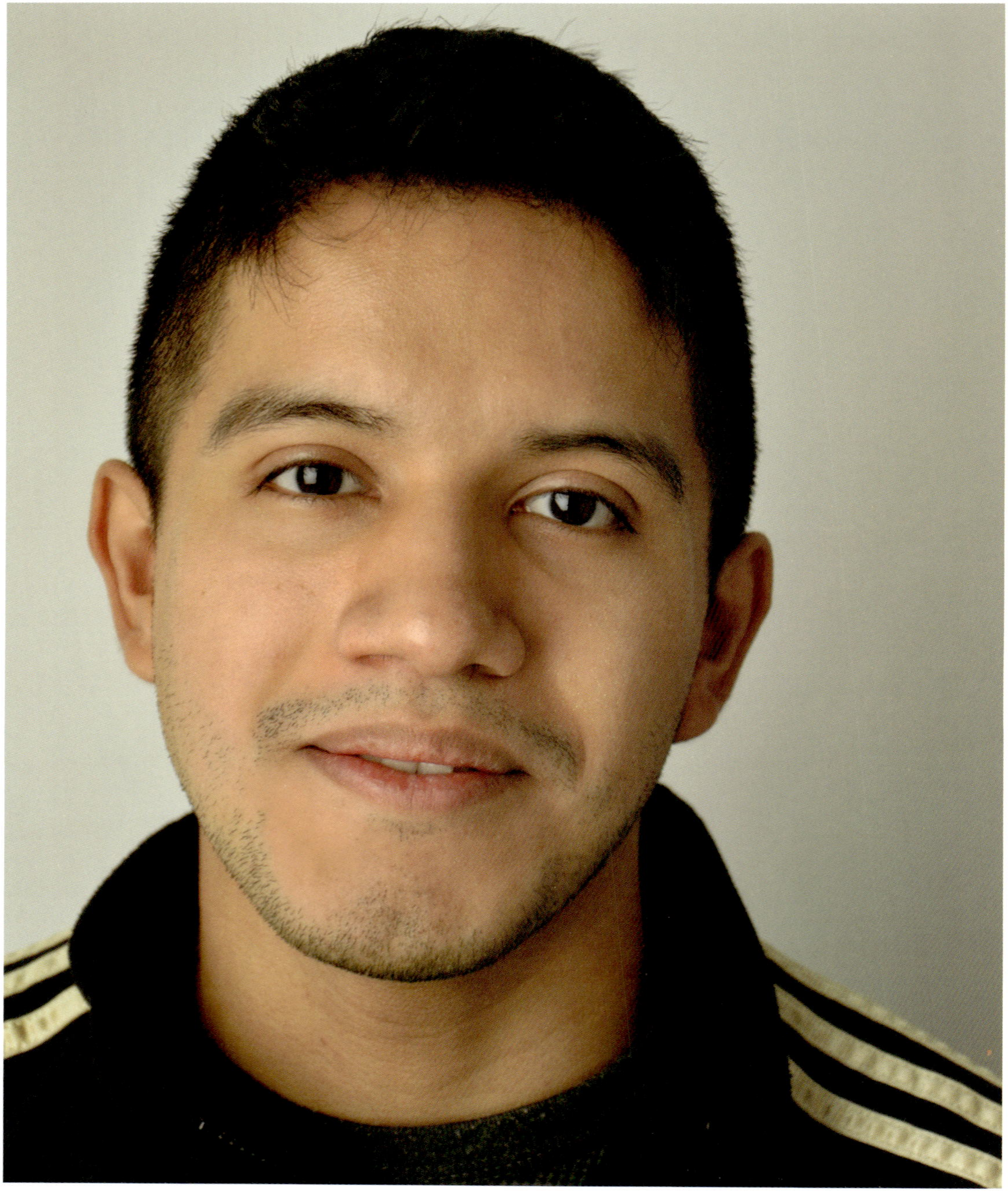

Abraham Morales
Photograph by Aaron Deming

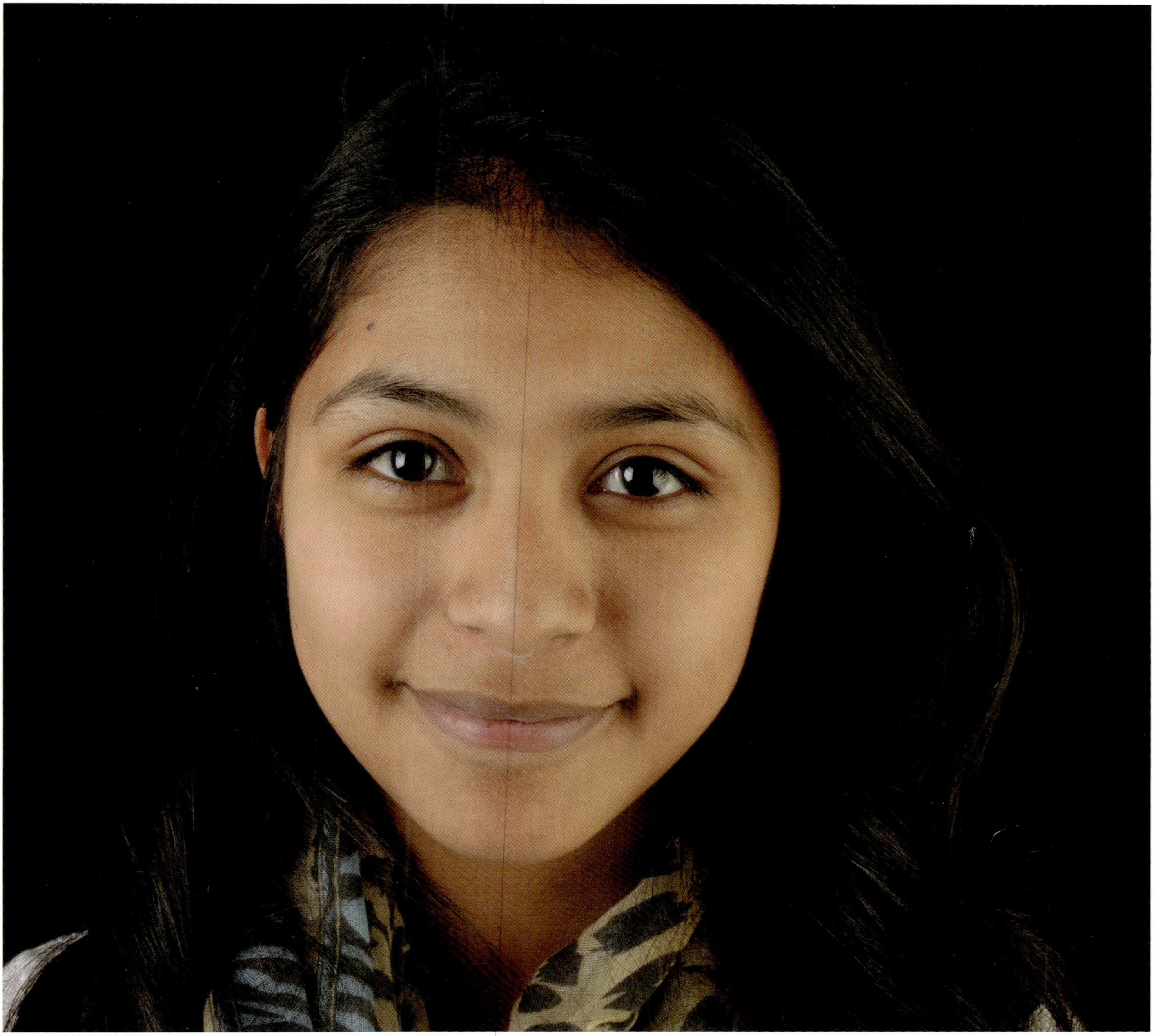

Luz Maria Camano-Rosales
Photograph by Aaron Deming

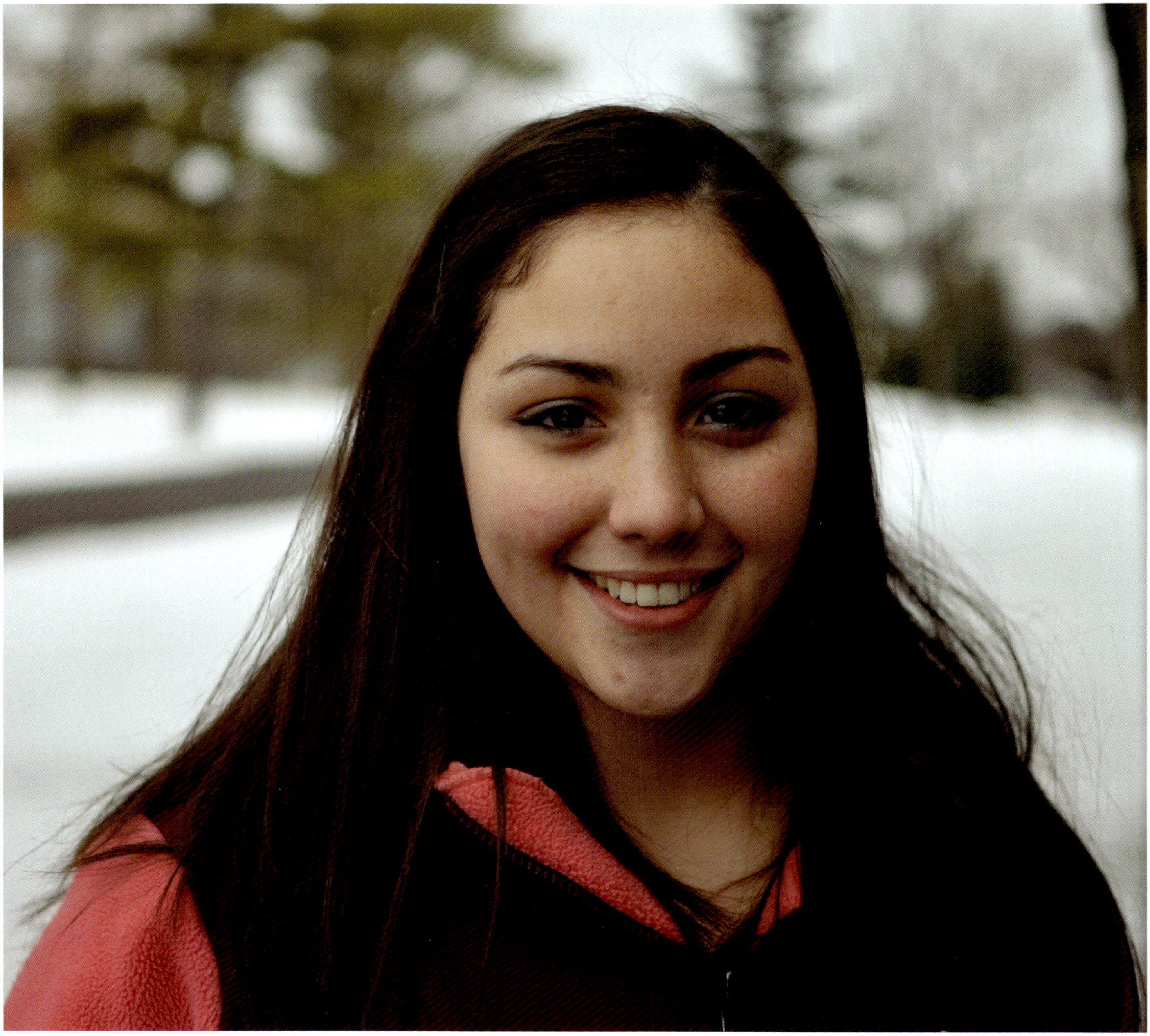

Jasmin Rodriguez
Photograph by Joshua F. Pitcher

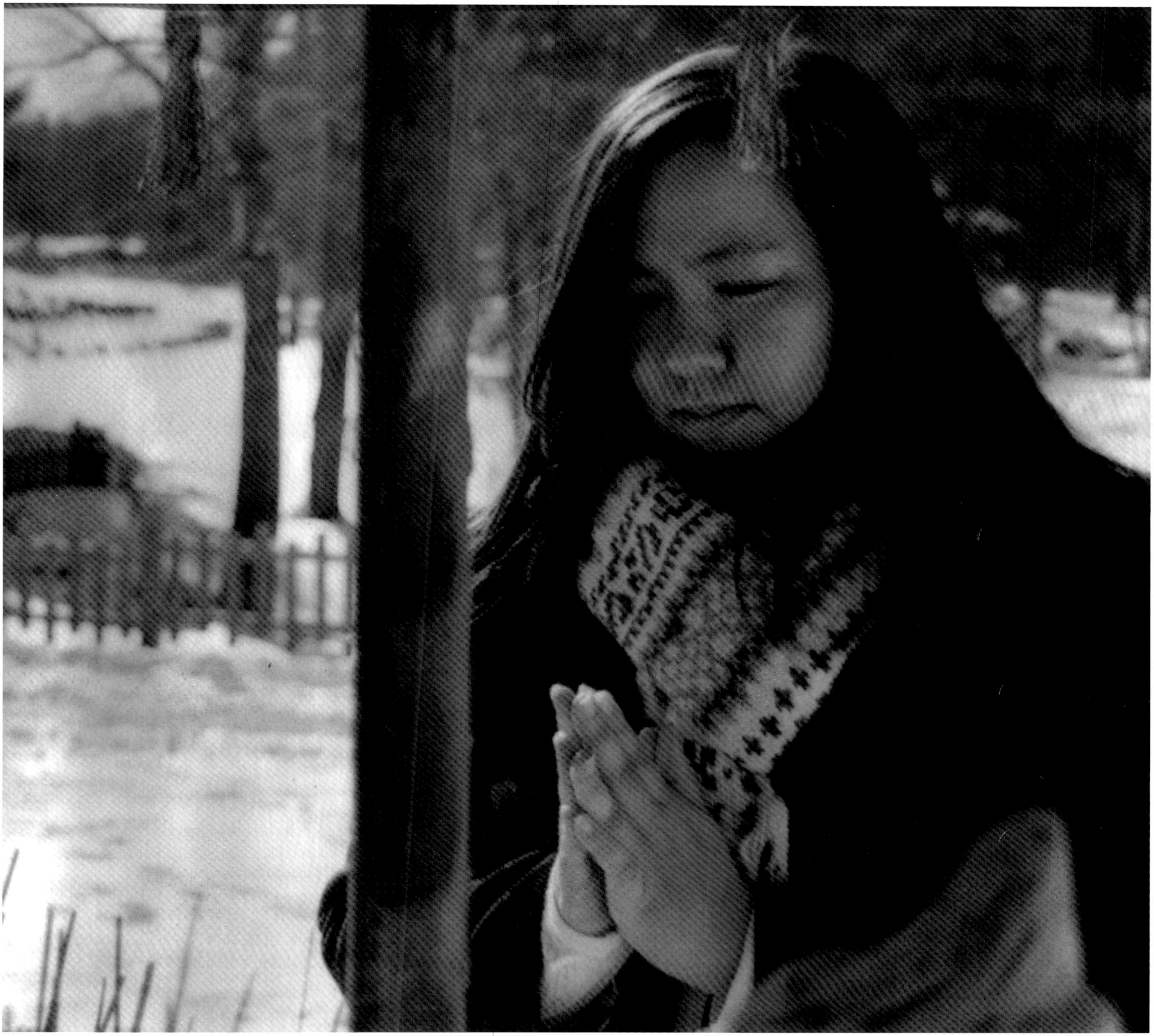

An Phan
Photograph by Wakana Yamada

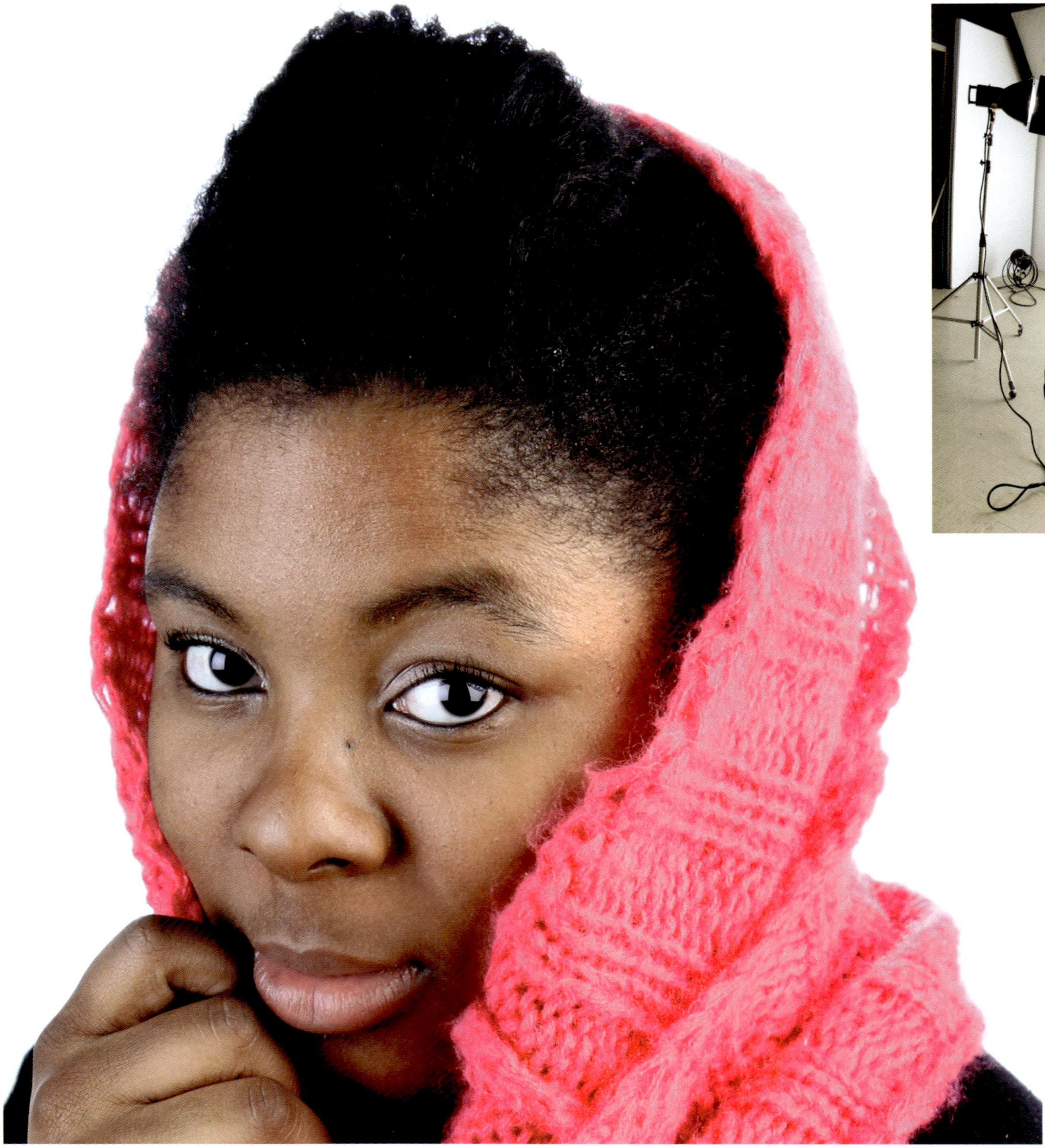

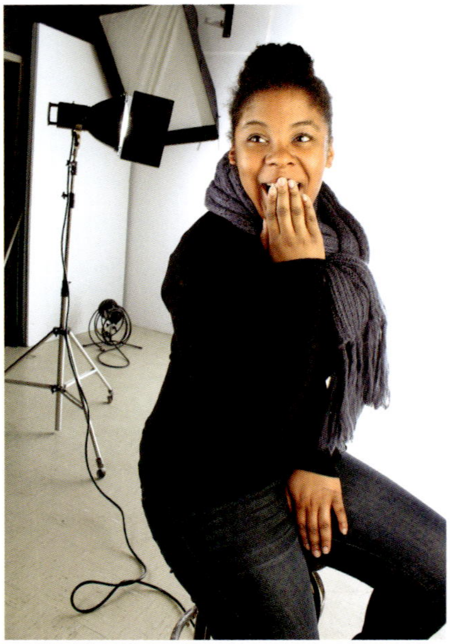

Sharhea Walters
Photographs by De'Anna Hopkinson

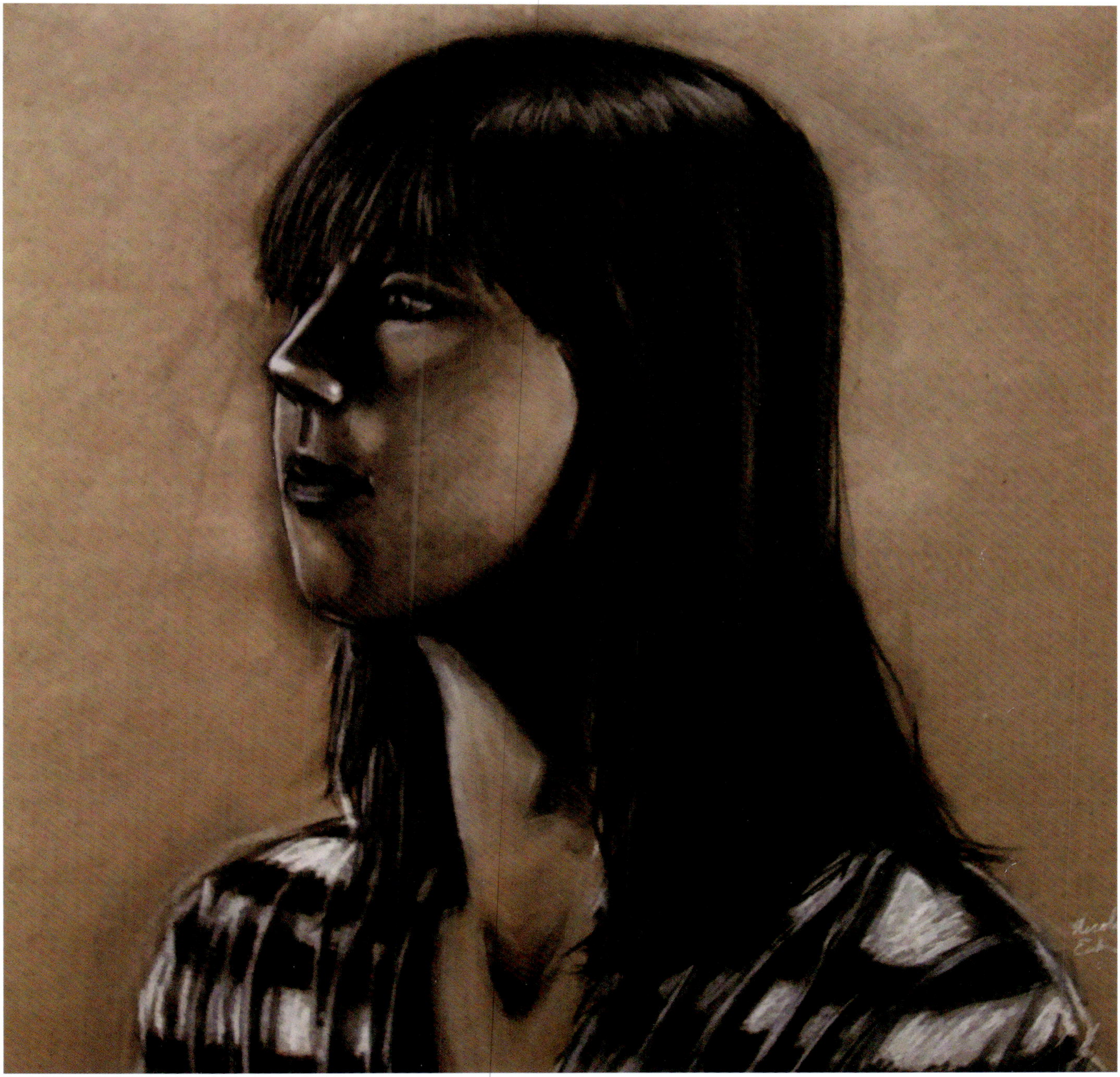

Samantha Smith
Drawing by Nicole Eakin

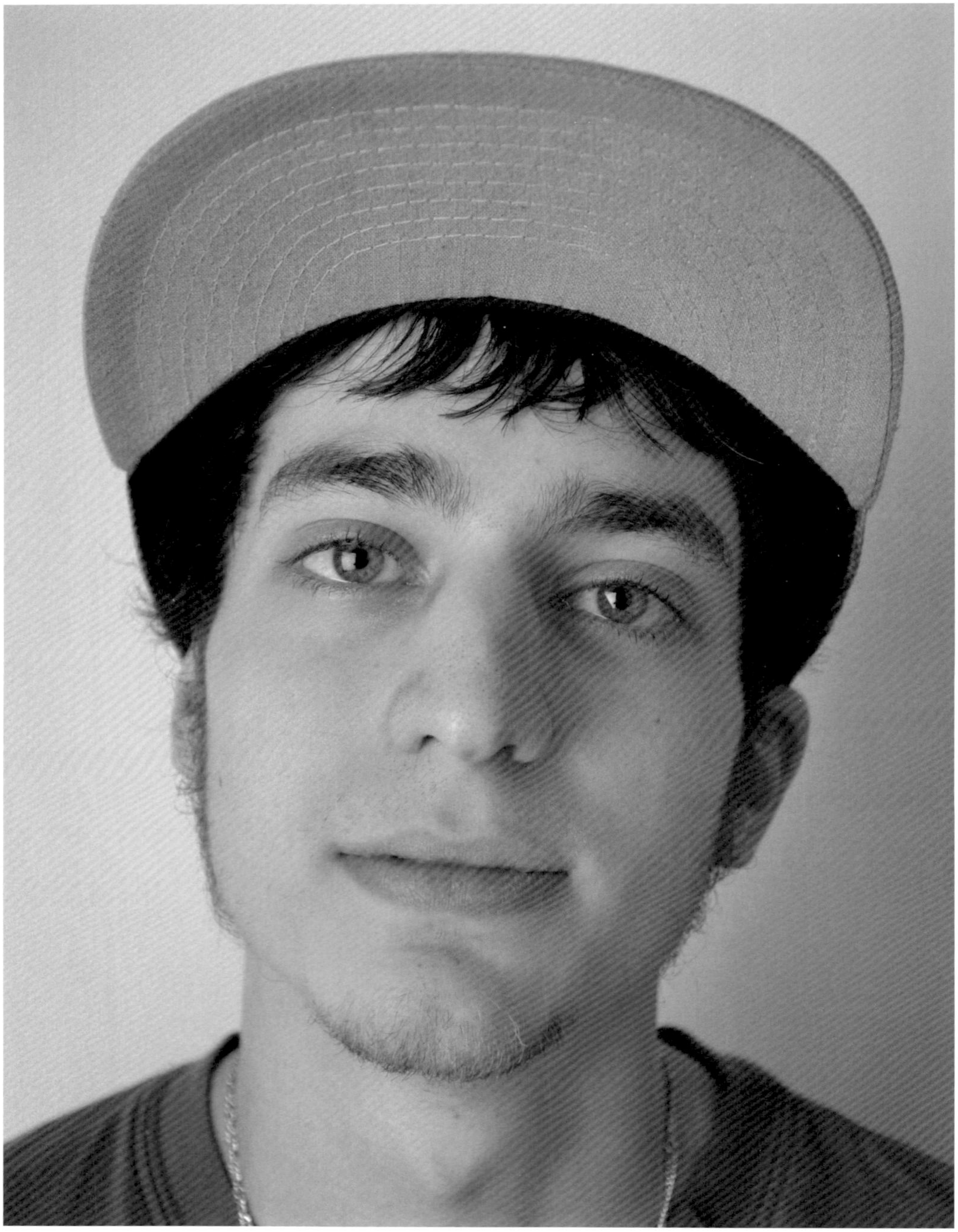

Caleb Mariano
Photograph by Aaron Deming

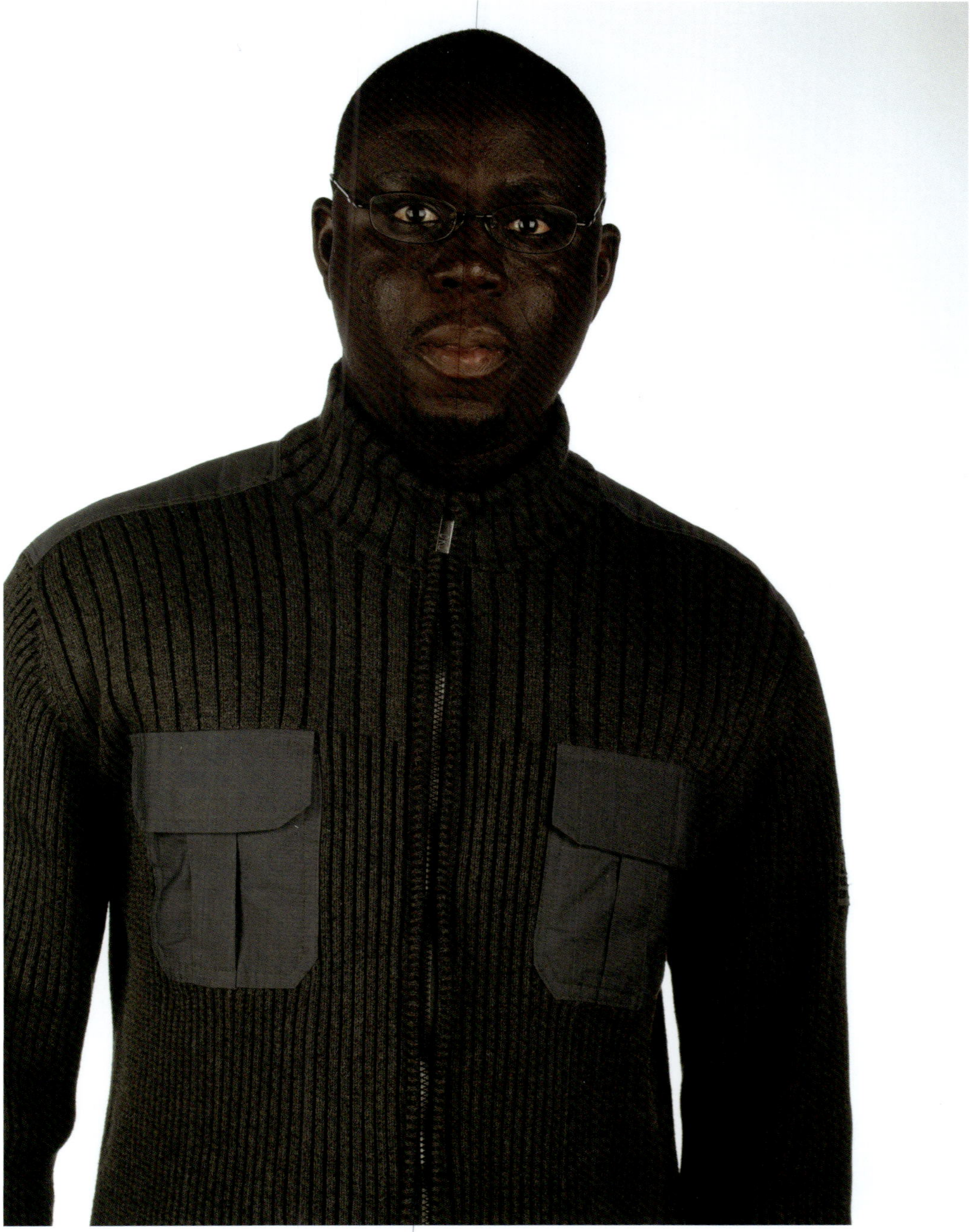

Cheikh Khouma
Photograph by Frederick F. Zang

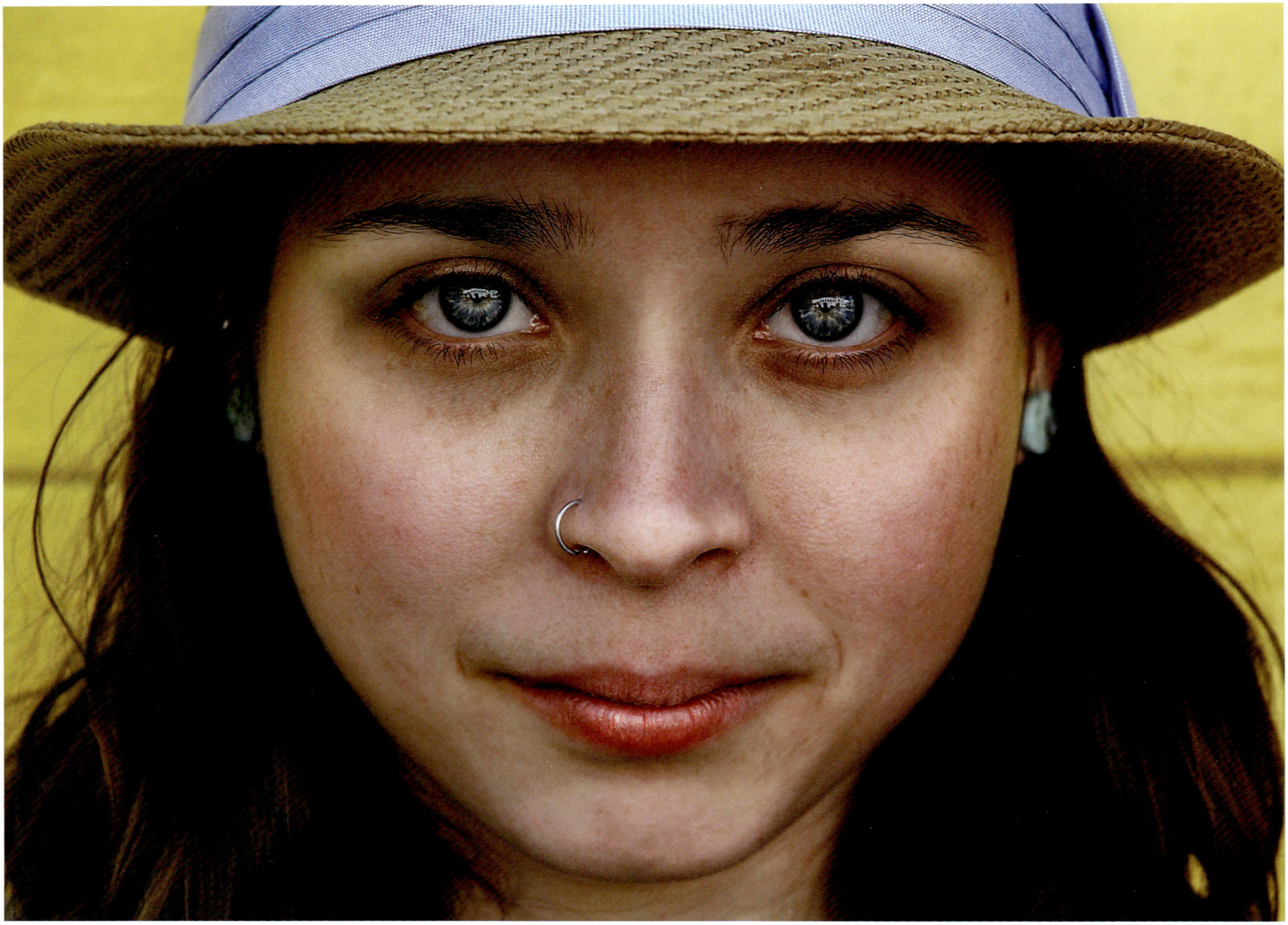

Ashley Meyers
Photograph by Shai Walters

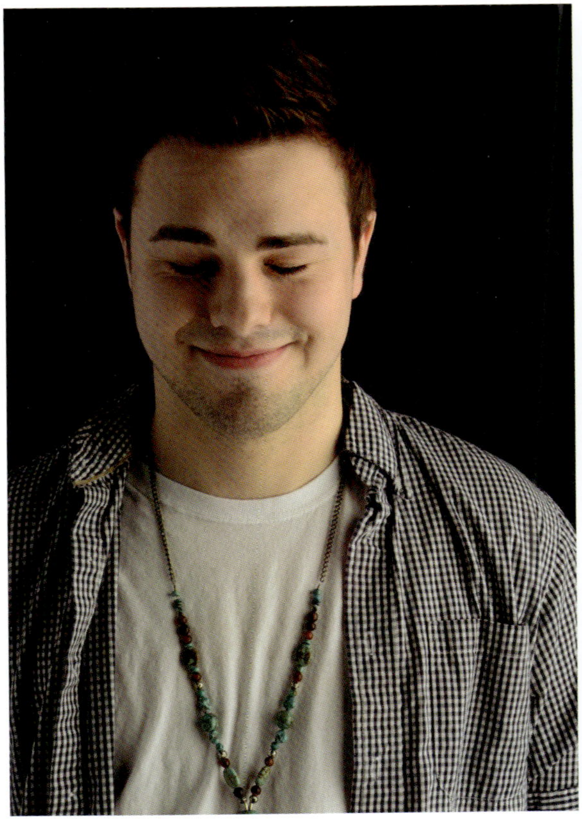

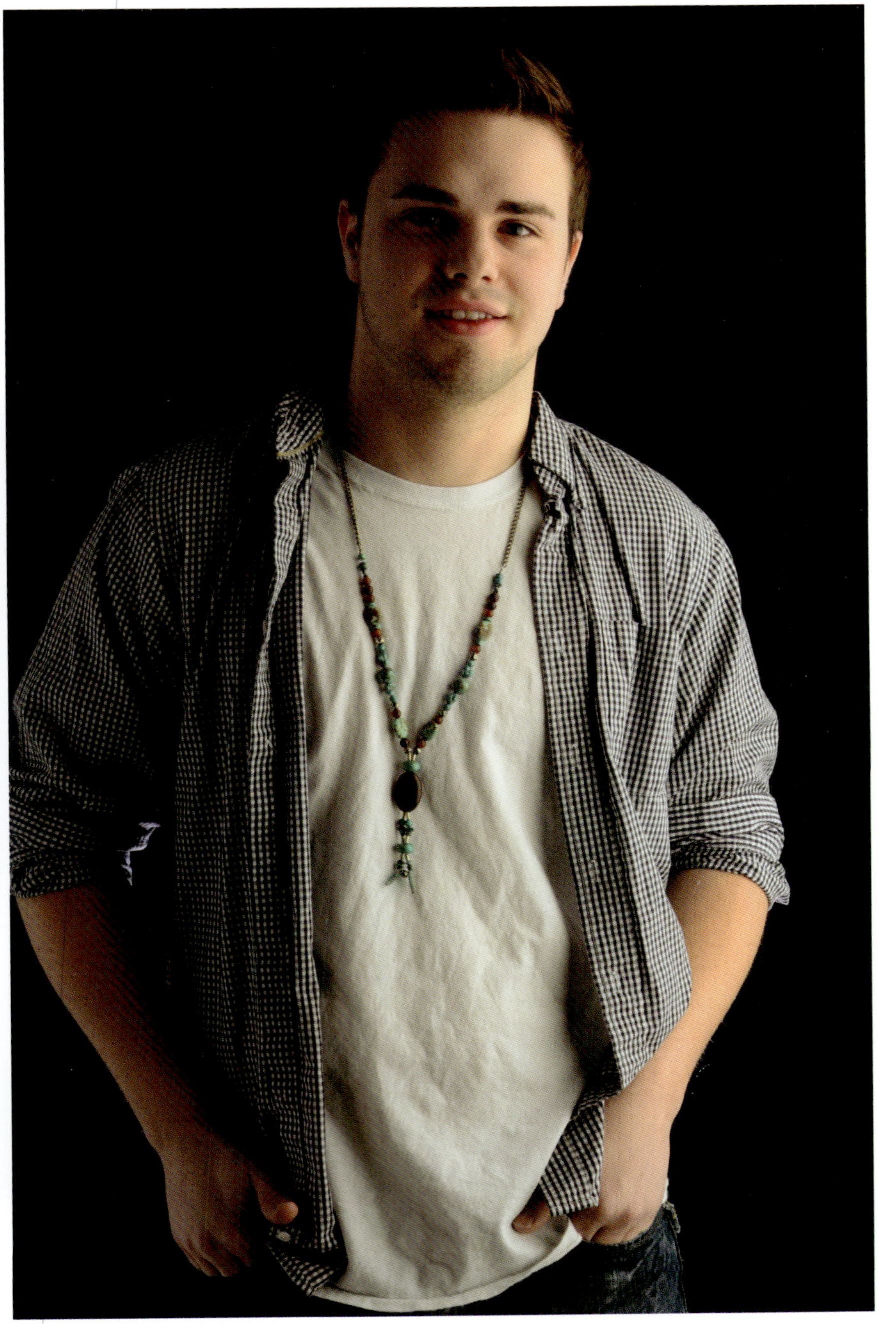

Jacob Dowker
Photograph by David Lloyd

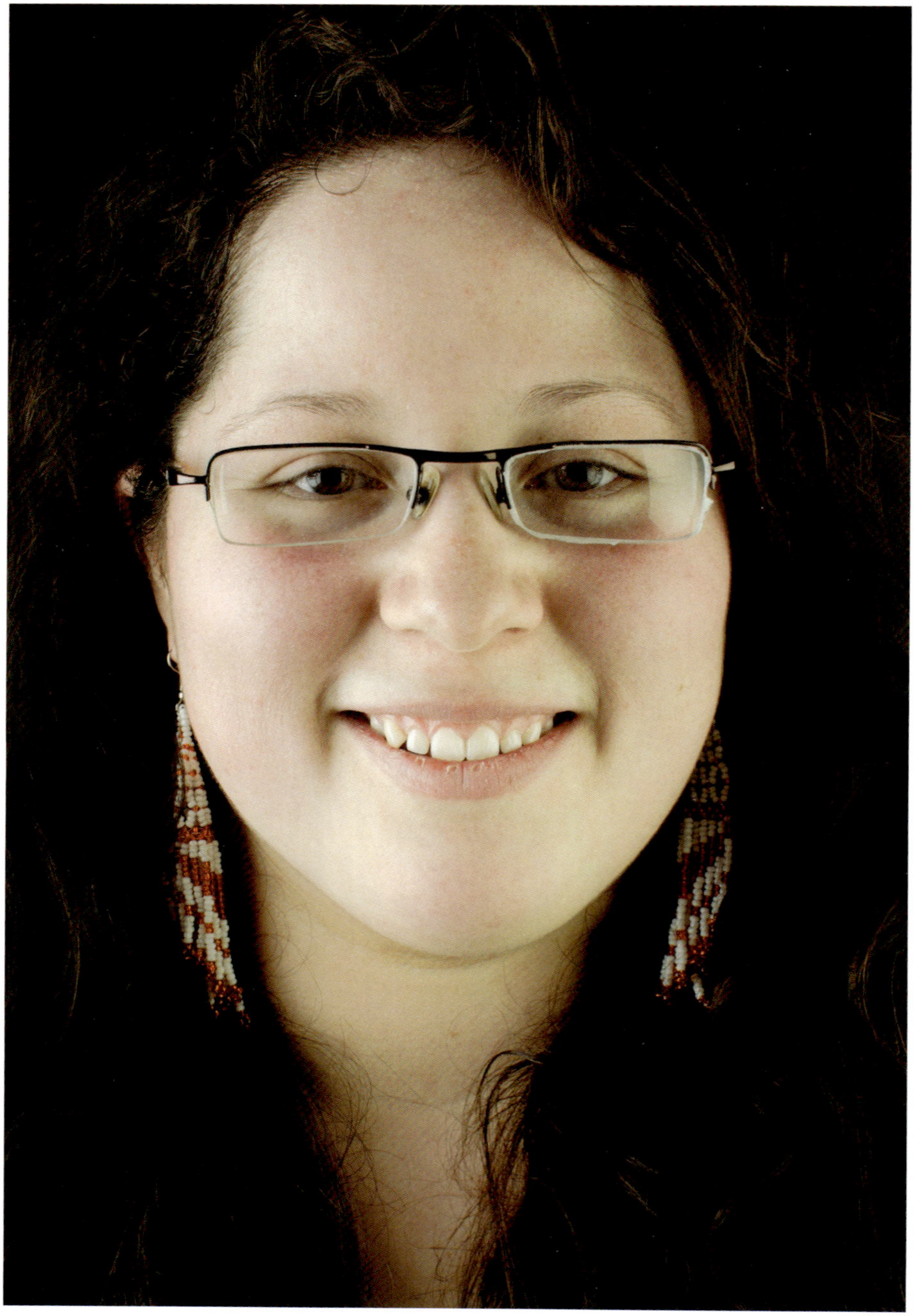

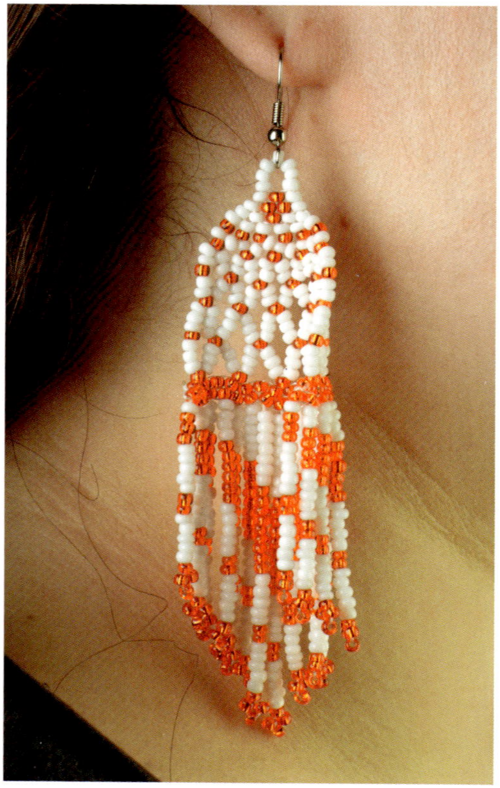

Jamie Teiewisahste Ransom

Photographs by Aaron Deming

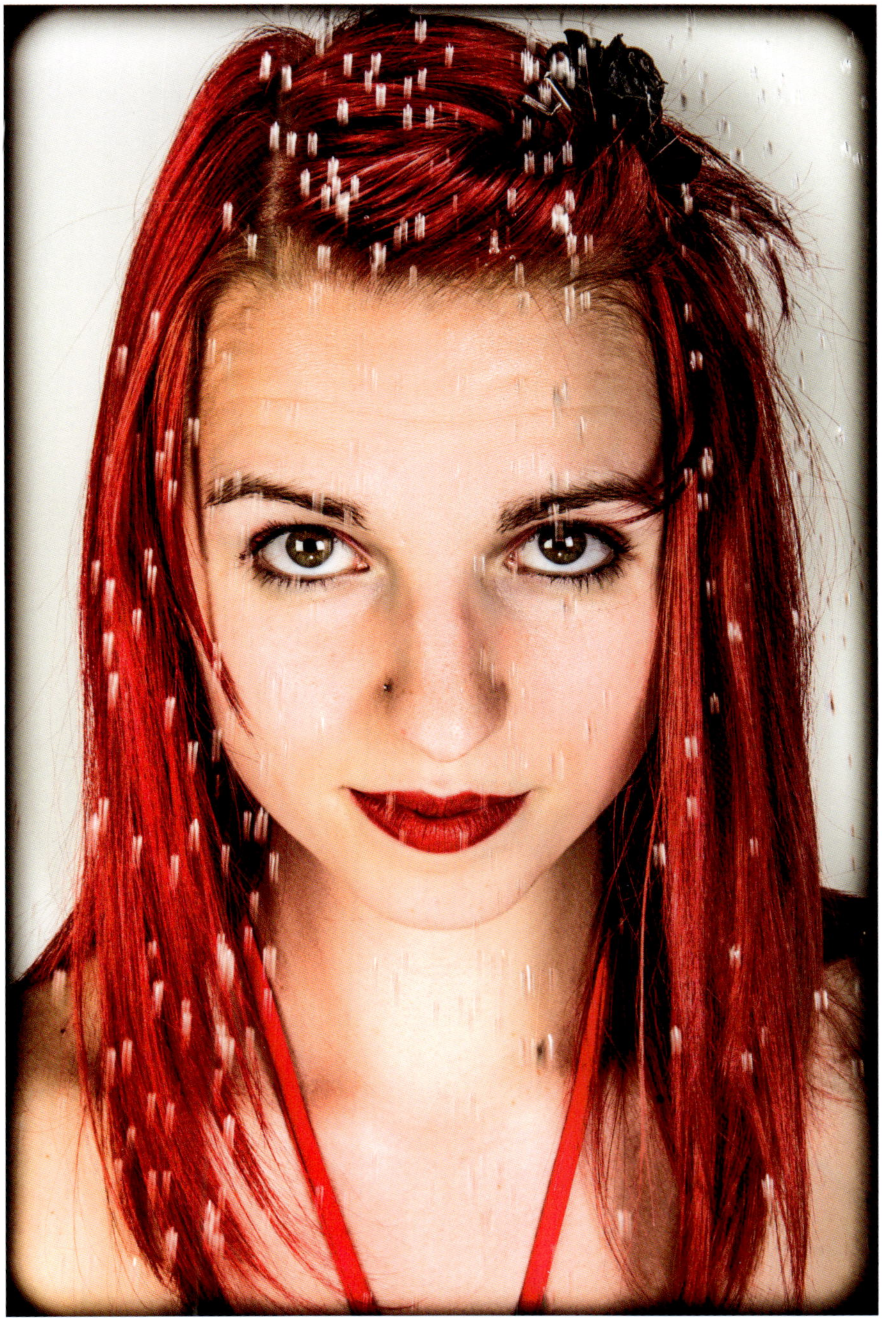

Katelyn Washburn
Photograph by Ross J. Deater

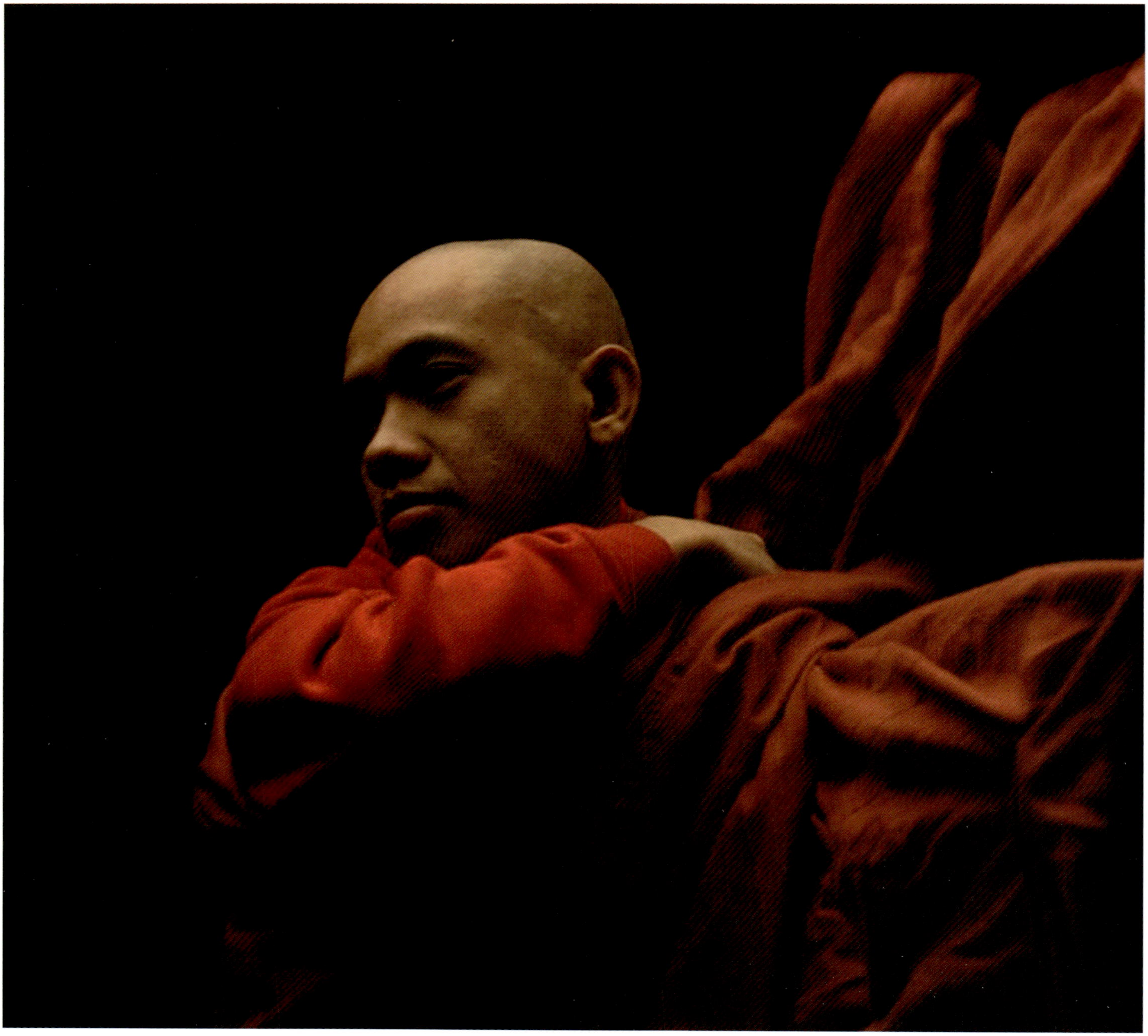

Agga Nyna
Photograph by Terry Burton

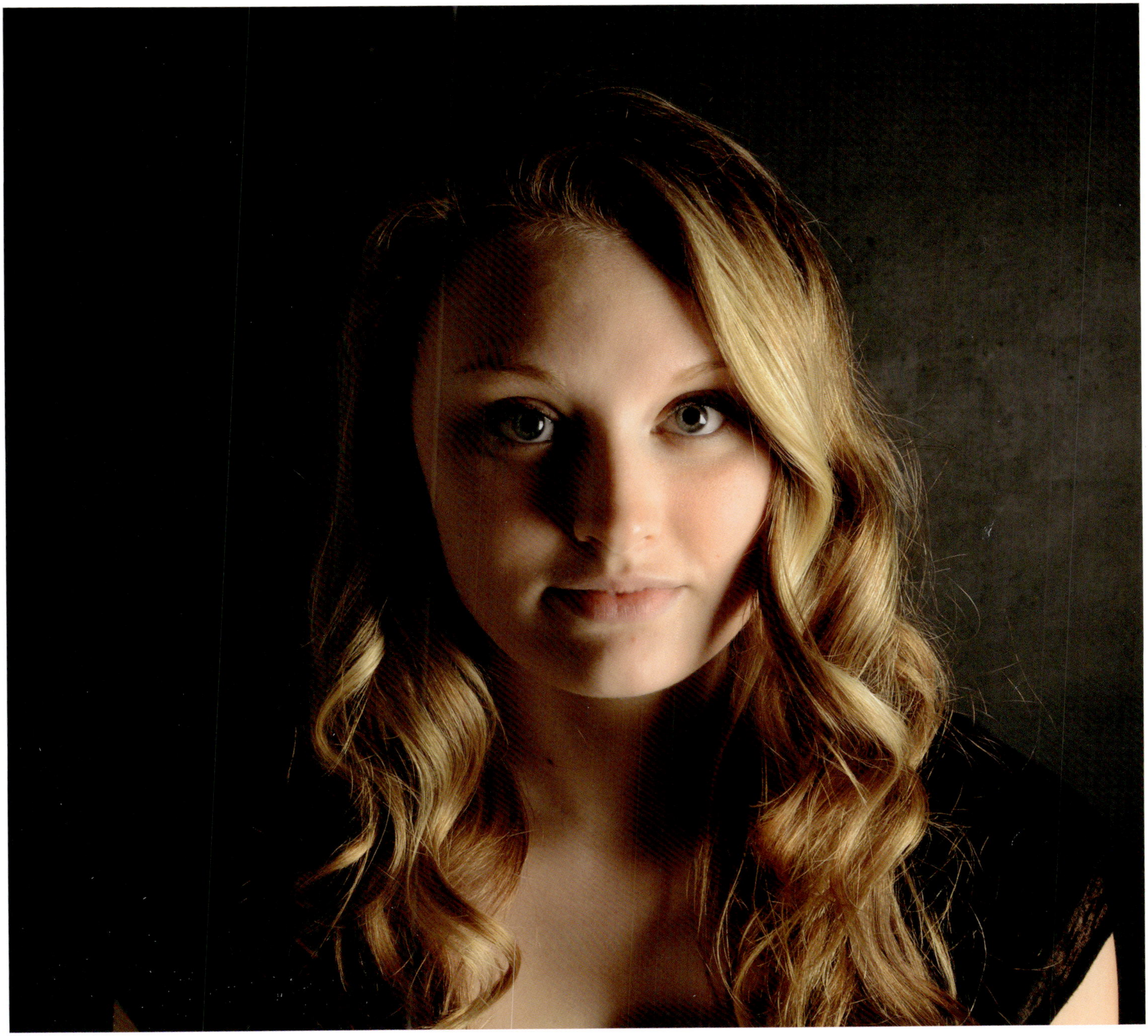

Lindsey Haskell
Photograph by Joshua F. Pitcher

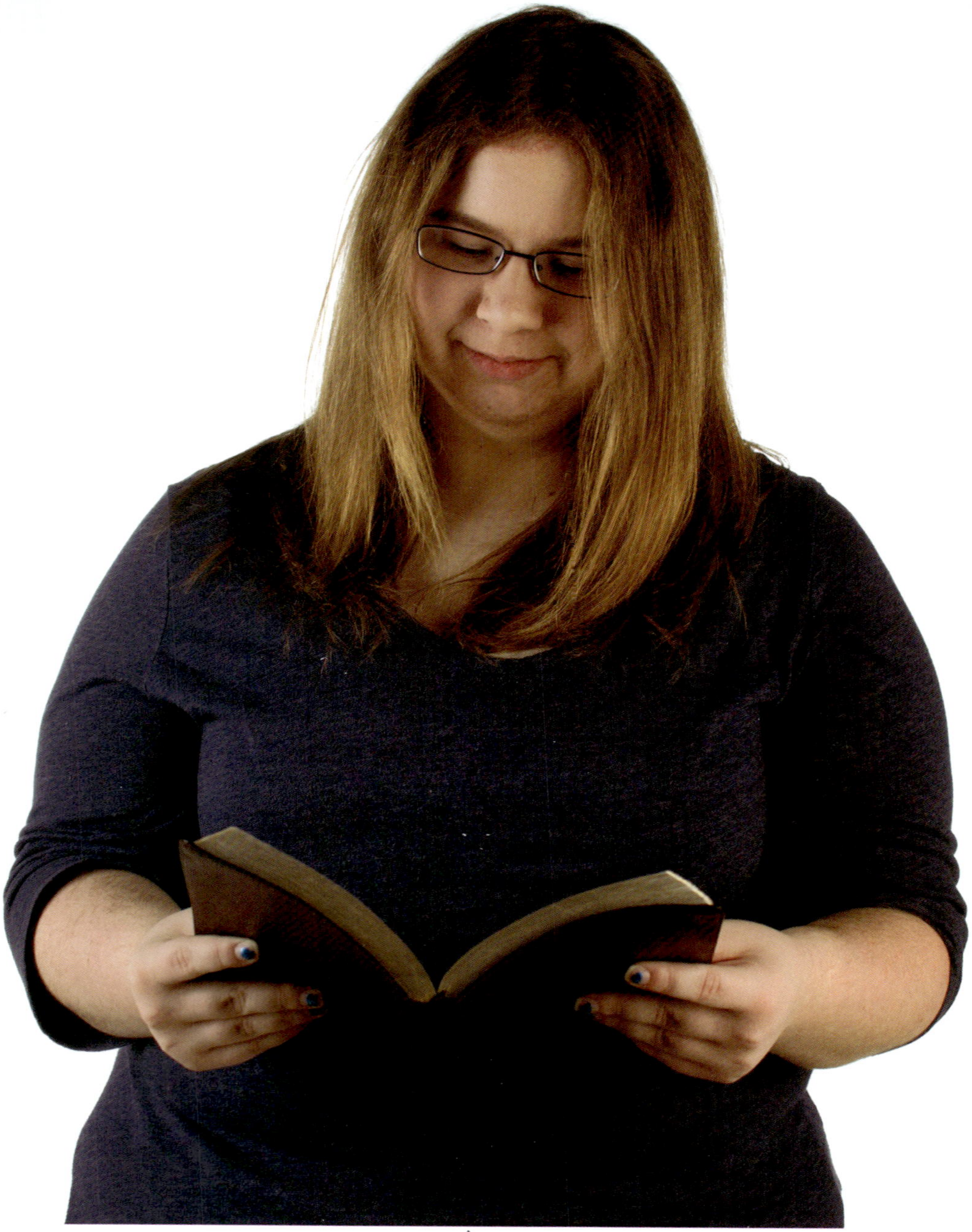

Sandra Warren
Photograph by Eden Richardson

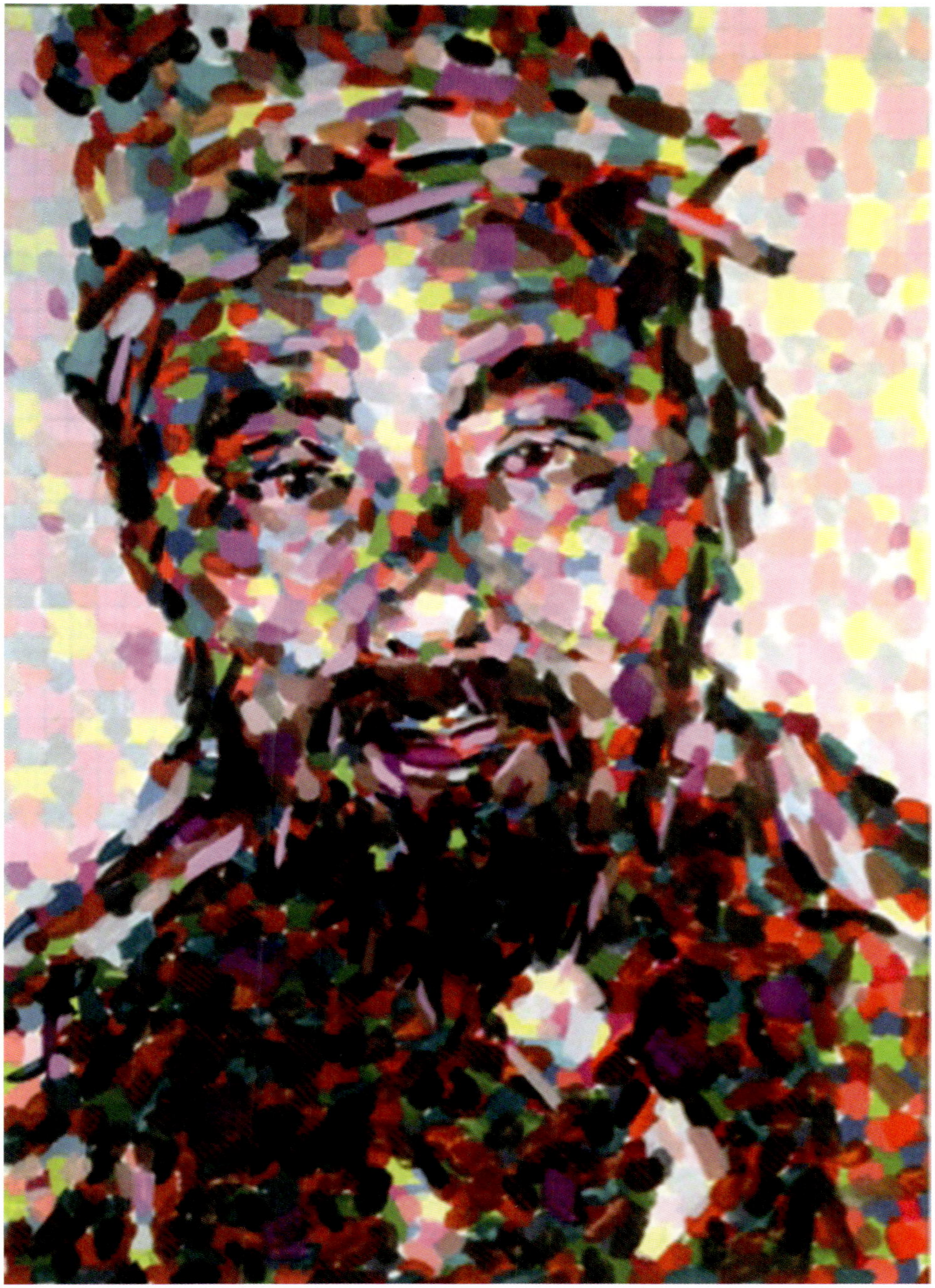

Rainbow Young
Painting by Jedediah Kimball

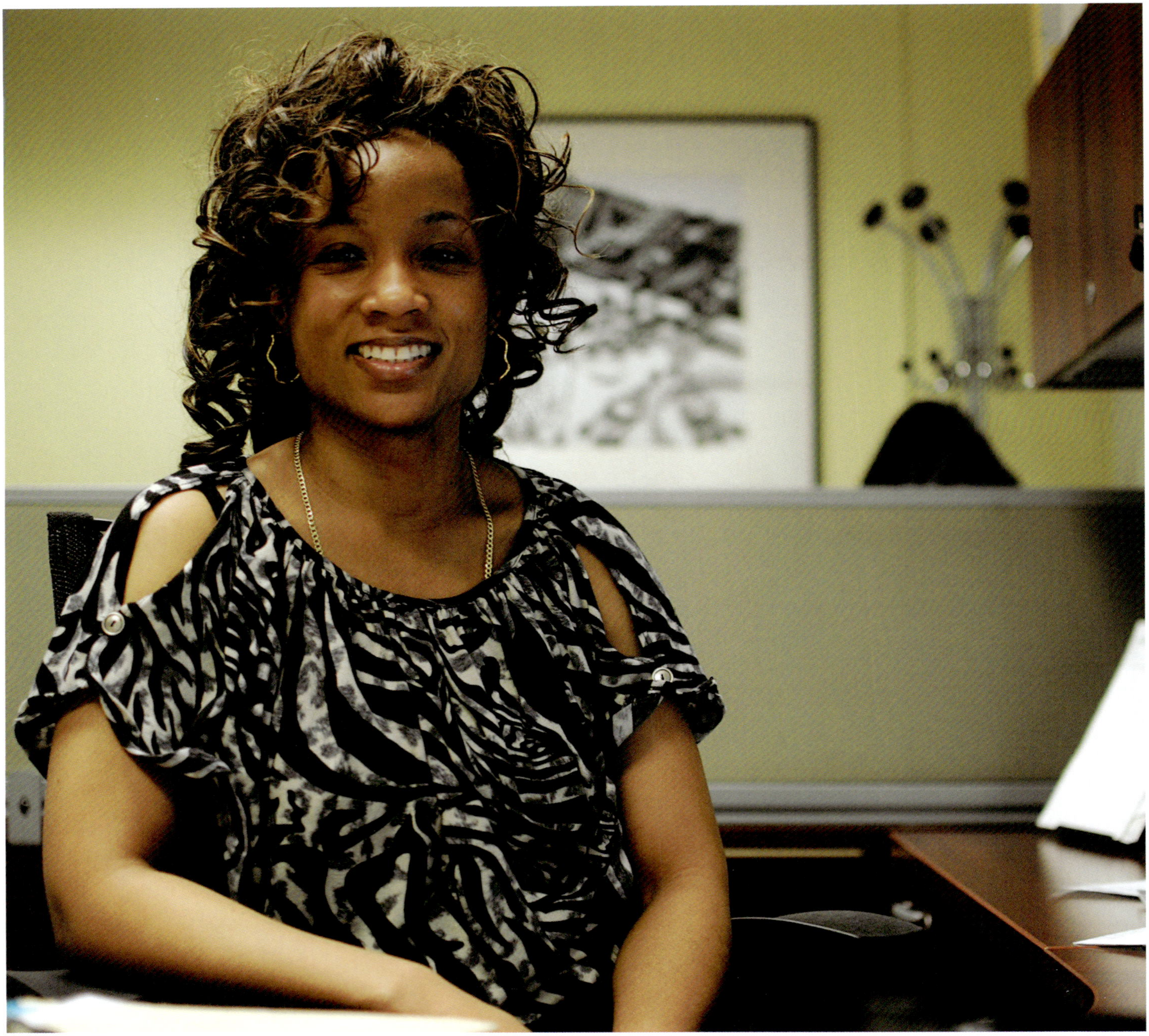

La Toya Richardson
Photograph by Frederick F. Zang

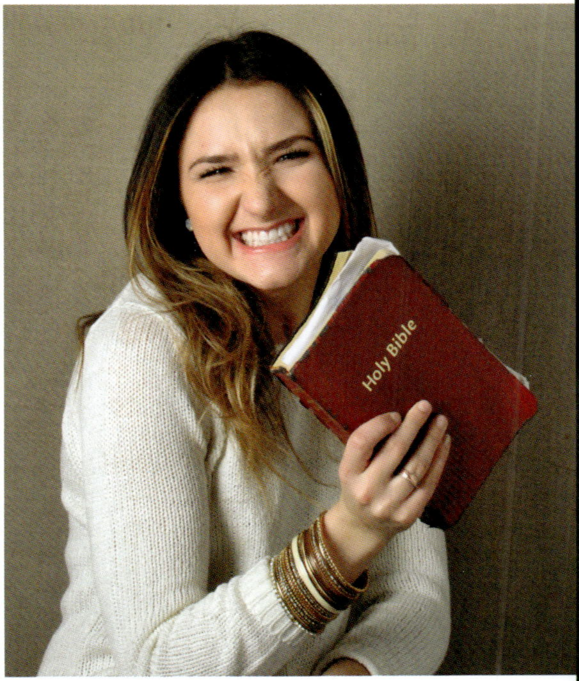

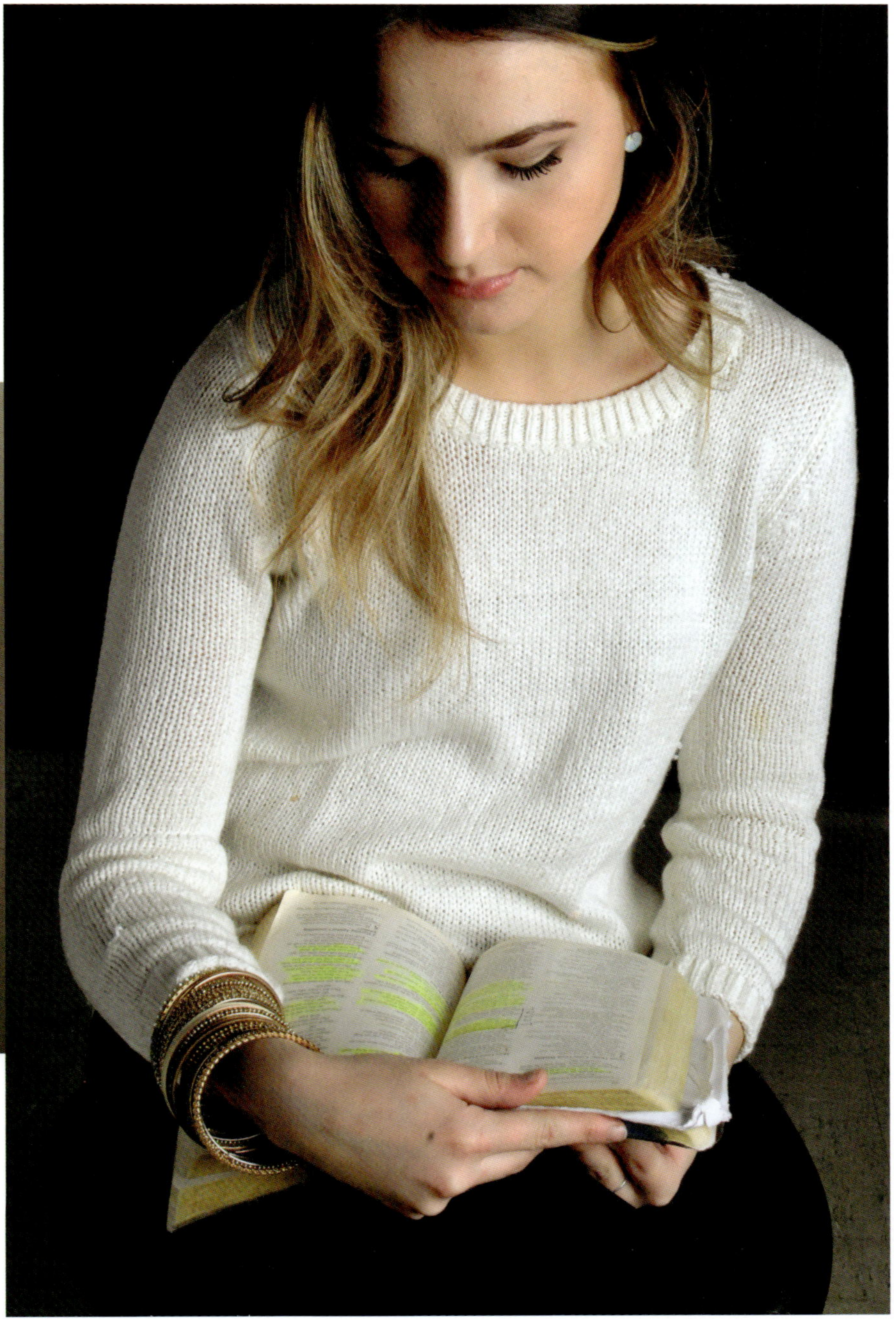

Casey McMichael
Photographs by Marsha Chamberlin Inuit Eyes

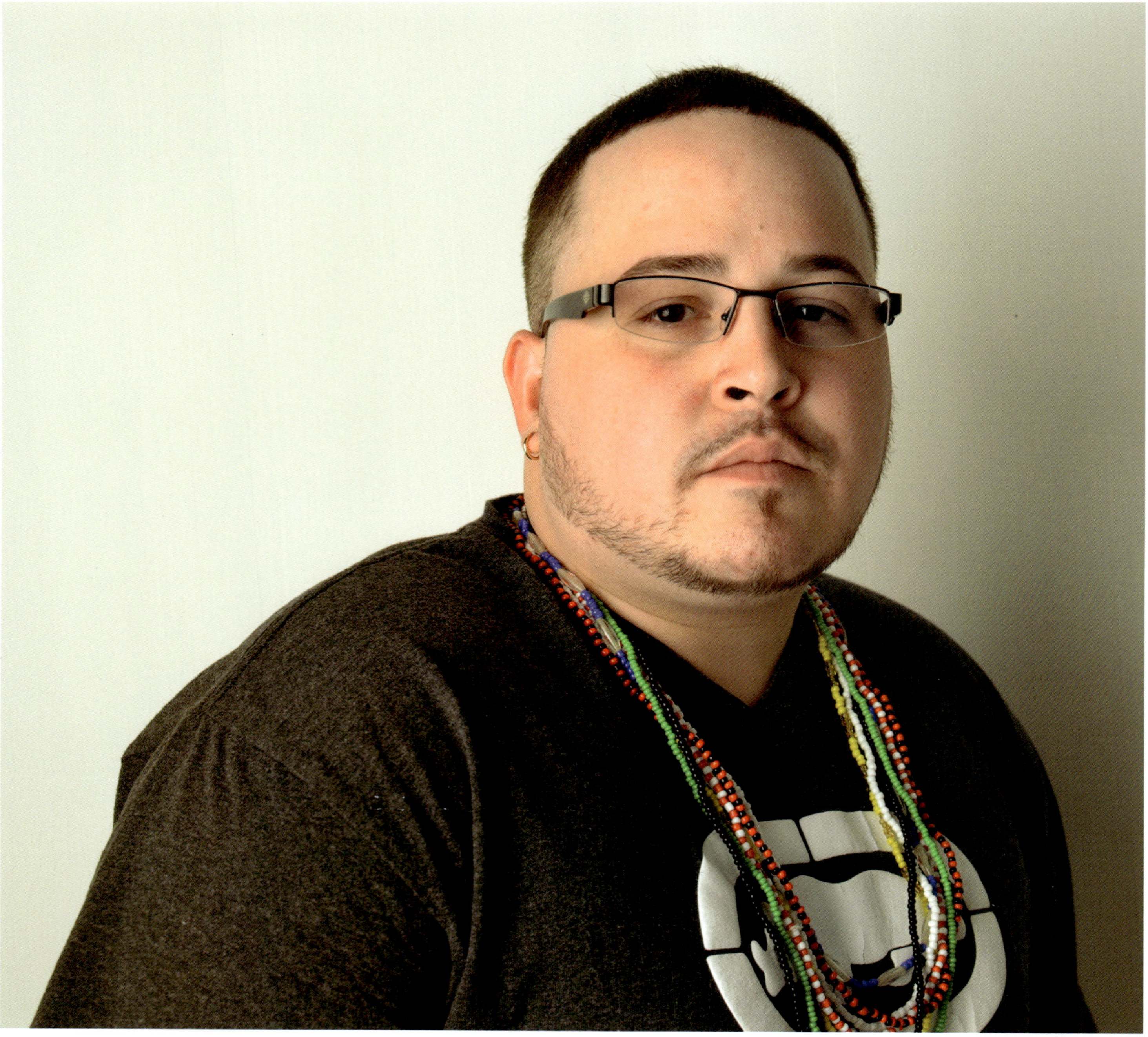

Alween Guivas
Photograph by Joshua F. Pitcher

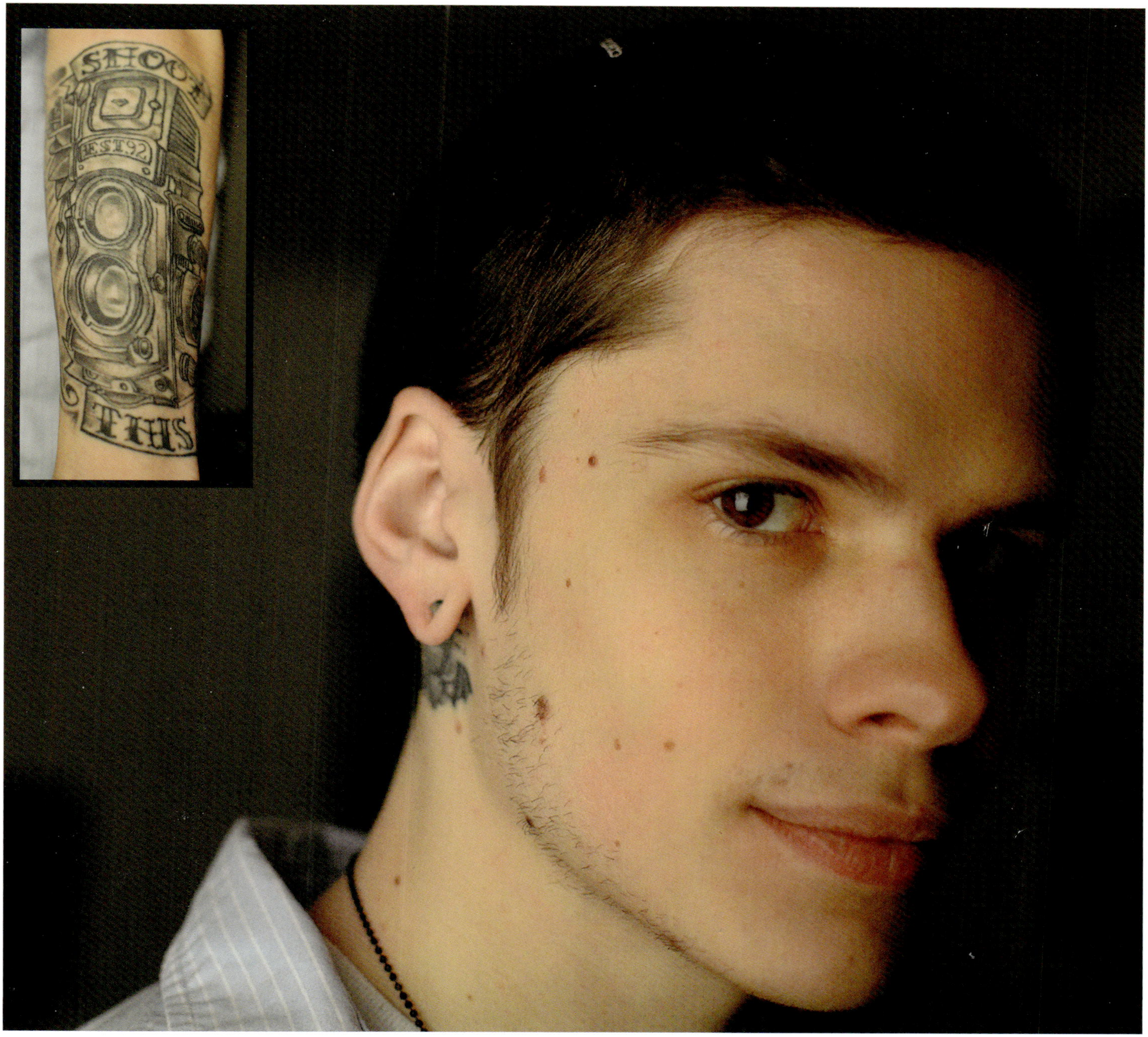

Frederick F. Zang

Photographs by Aaron Deming

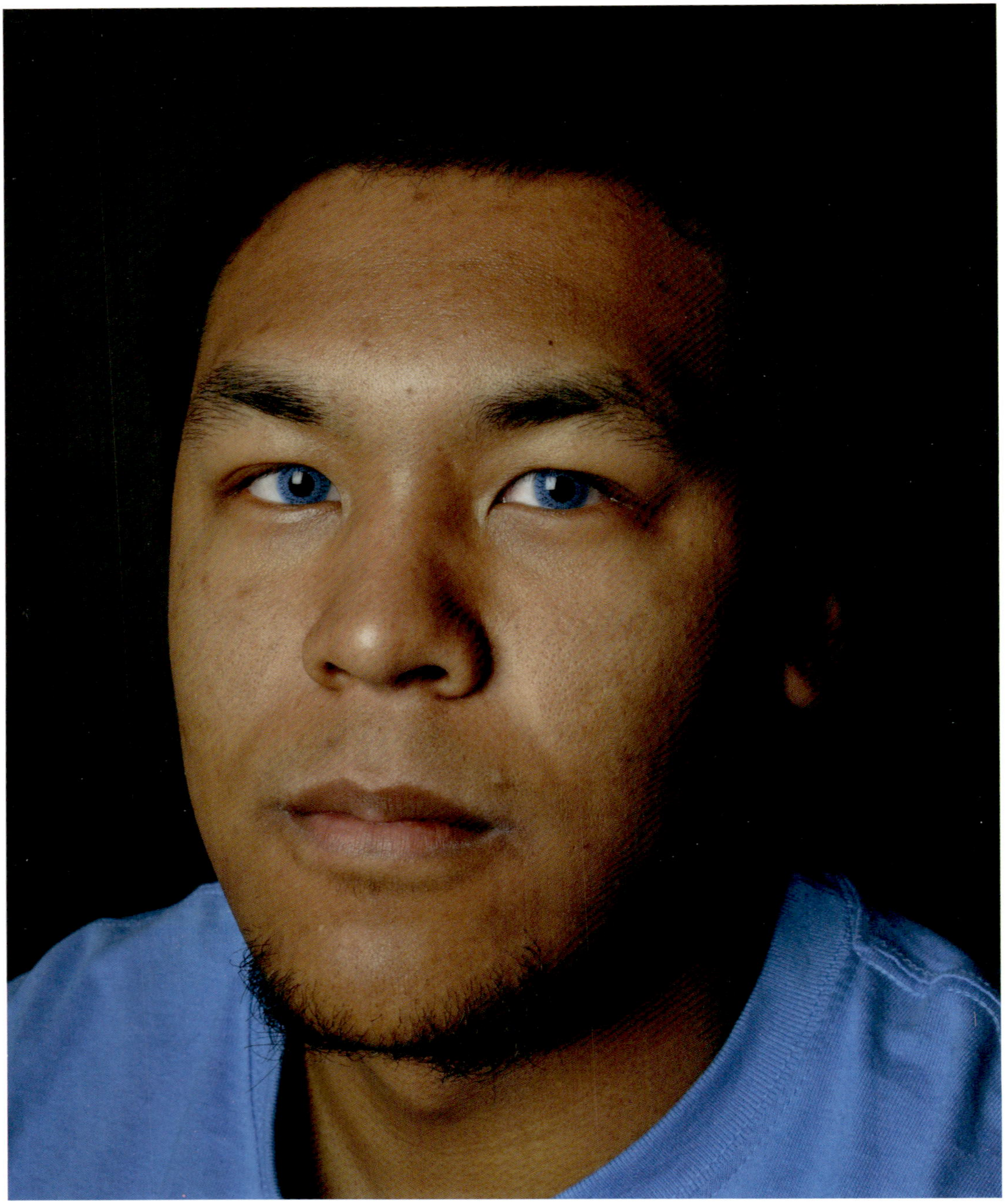

Zachary Miller
Photograph by Aaron Deming

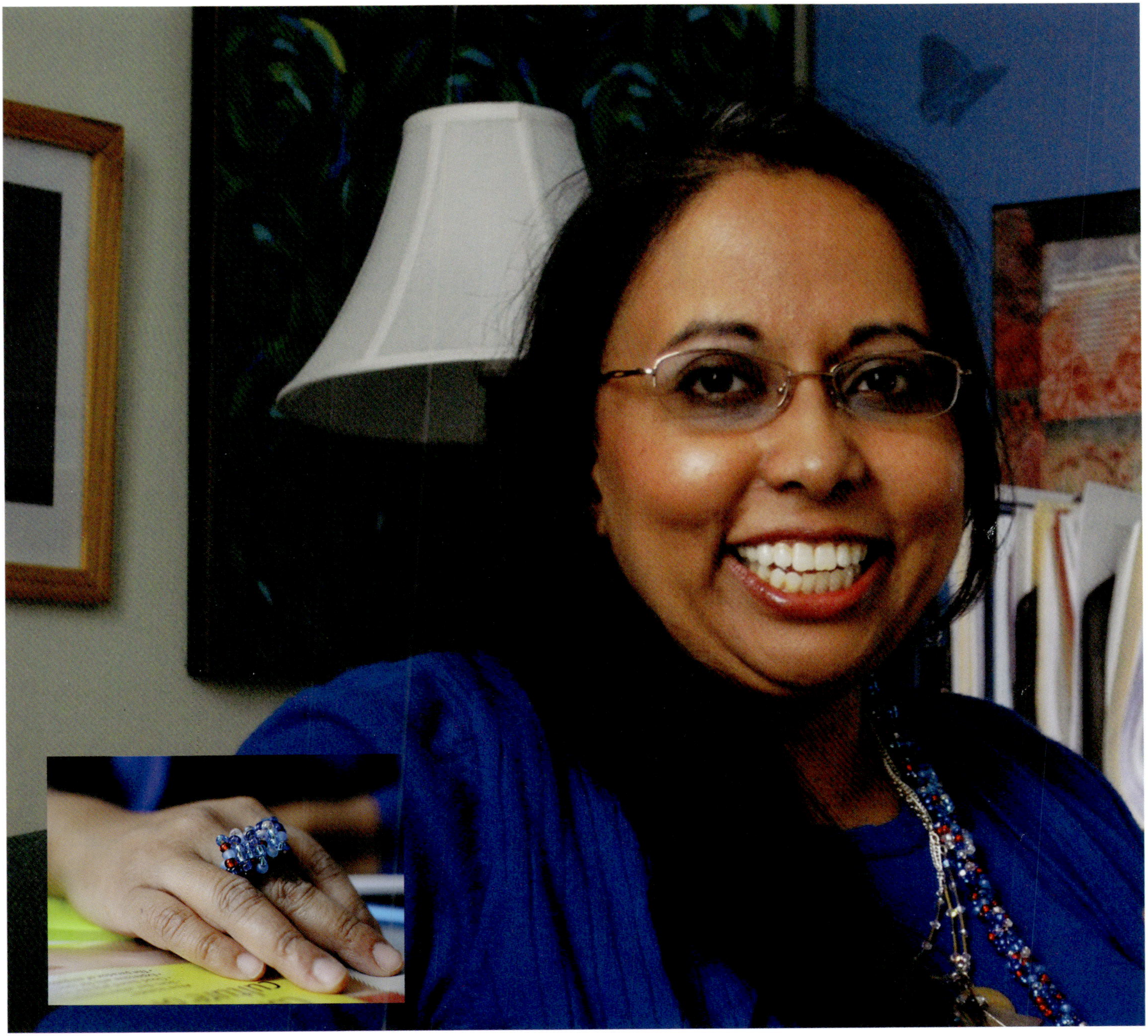

Maimun Khan

Photographs by Brigitta Field and Frederick F Zang

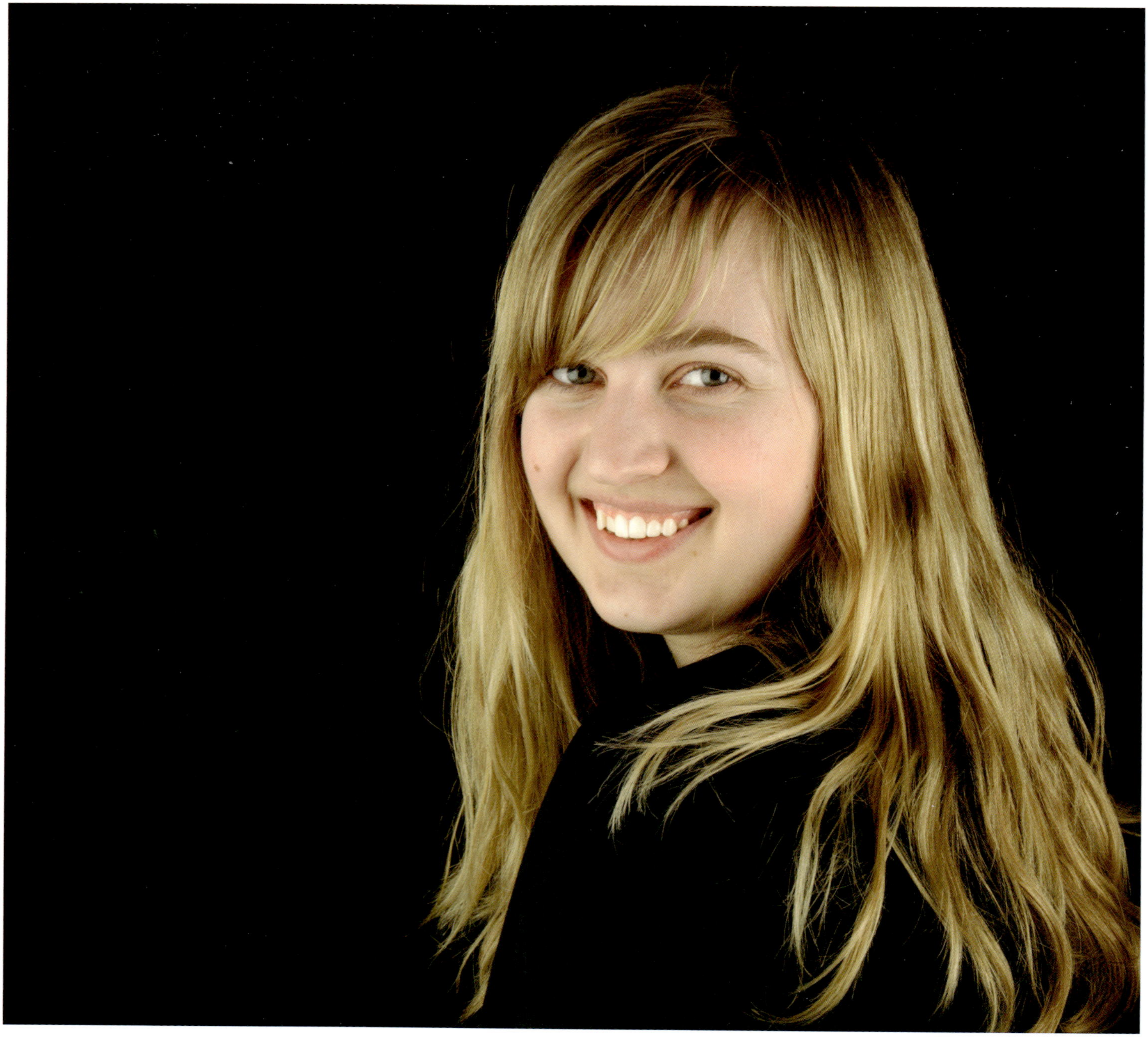

Brigitta Field
Photograph by Joshua F. Pitcher

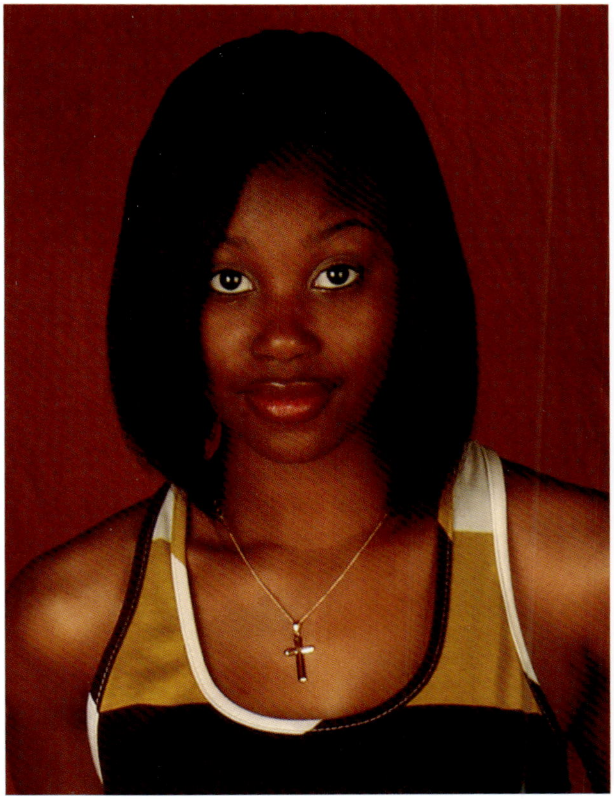

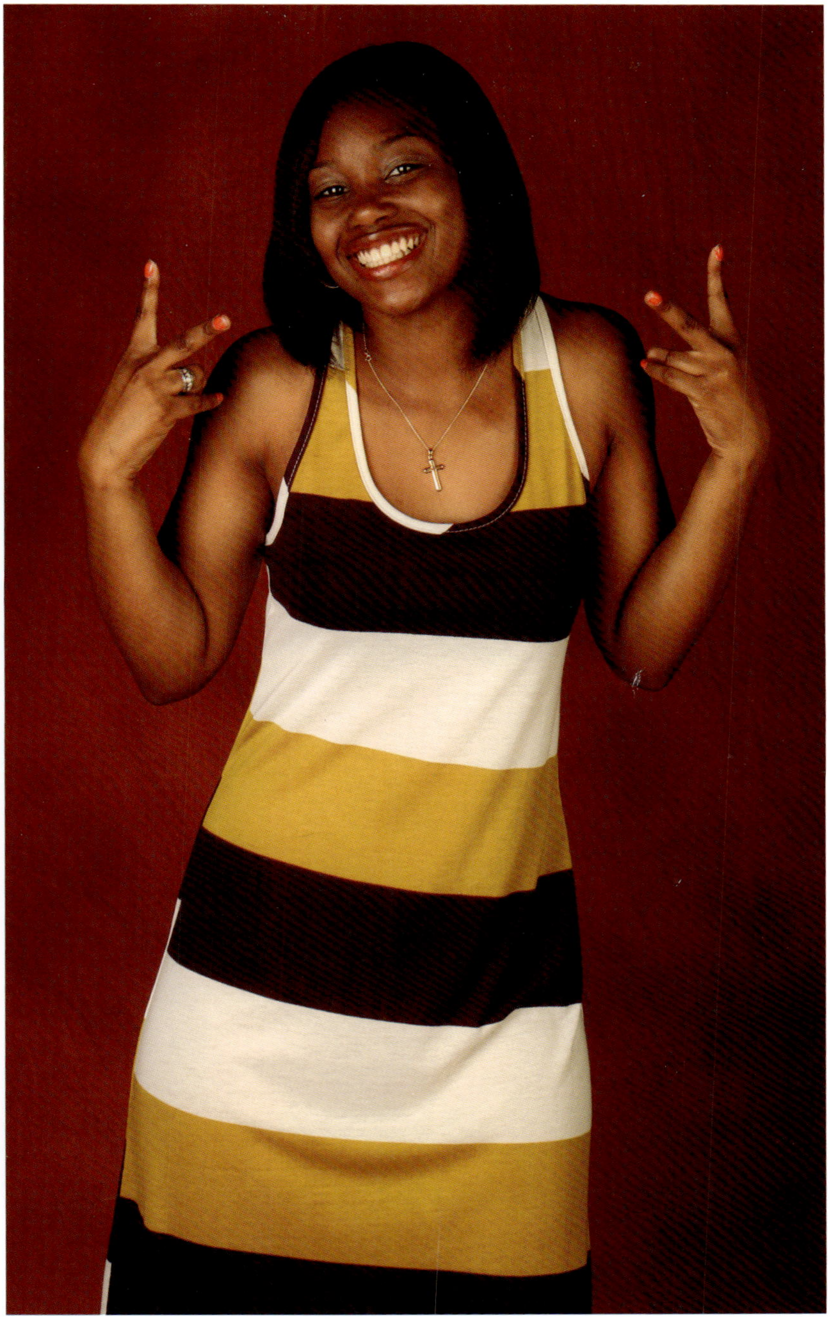

Diamond Young
Photograph by Shai Walters

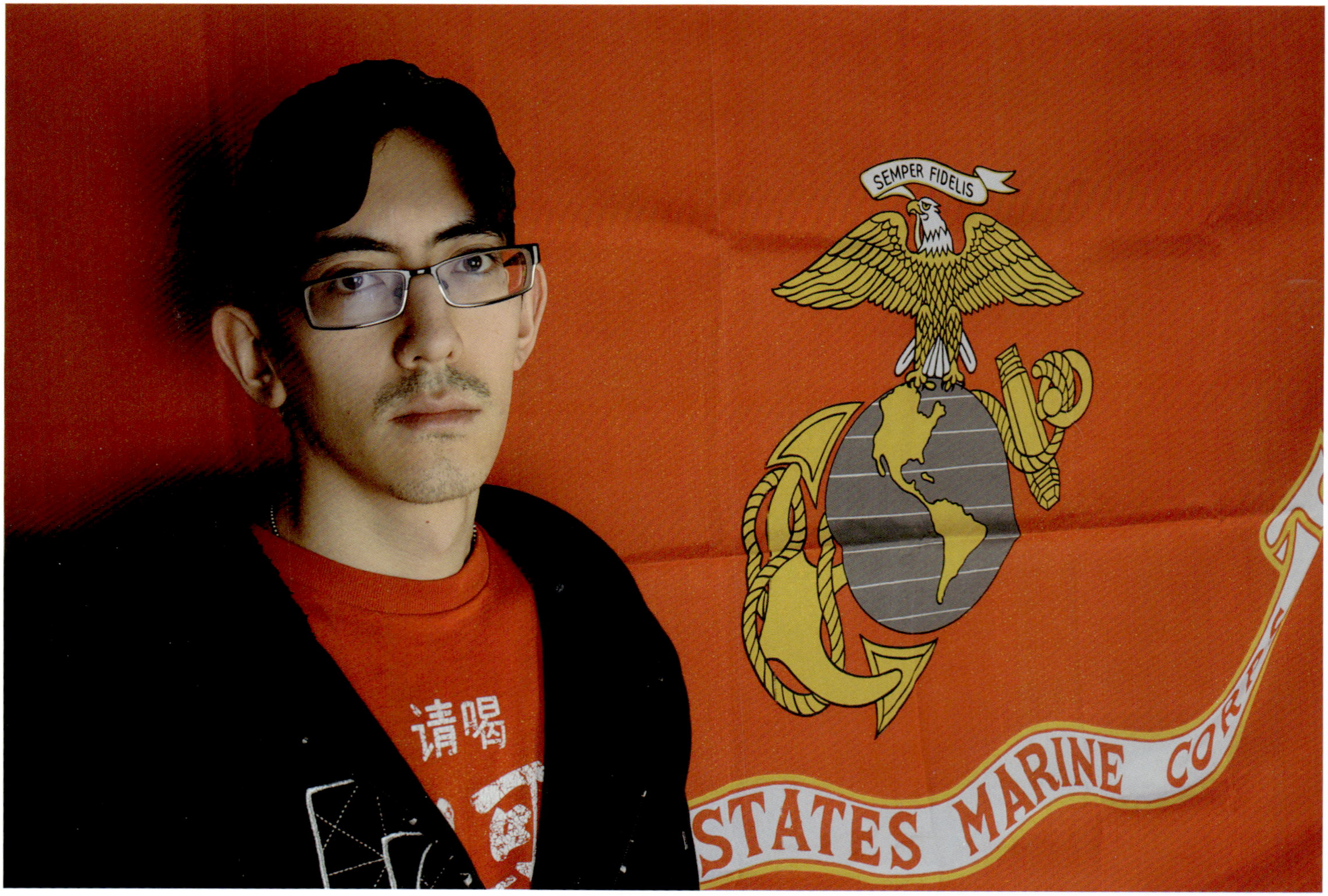

Sean Hugo
Photograph by Joshua F. Pitcher

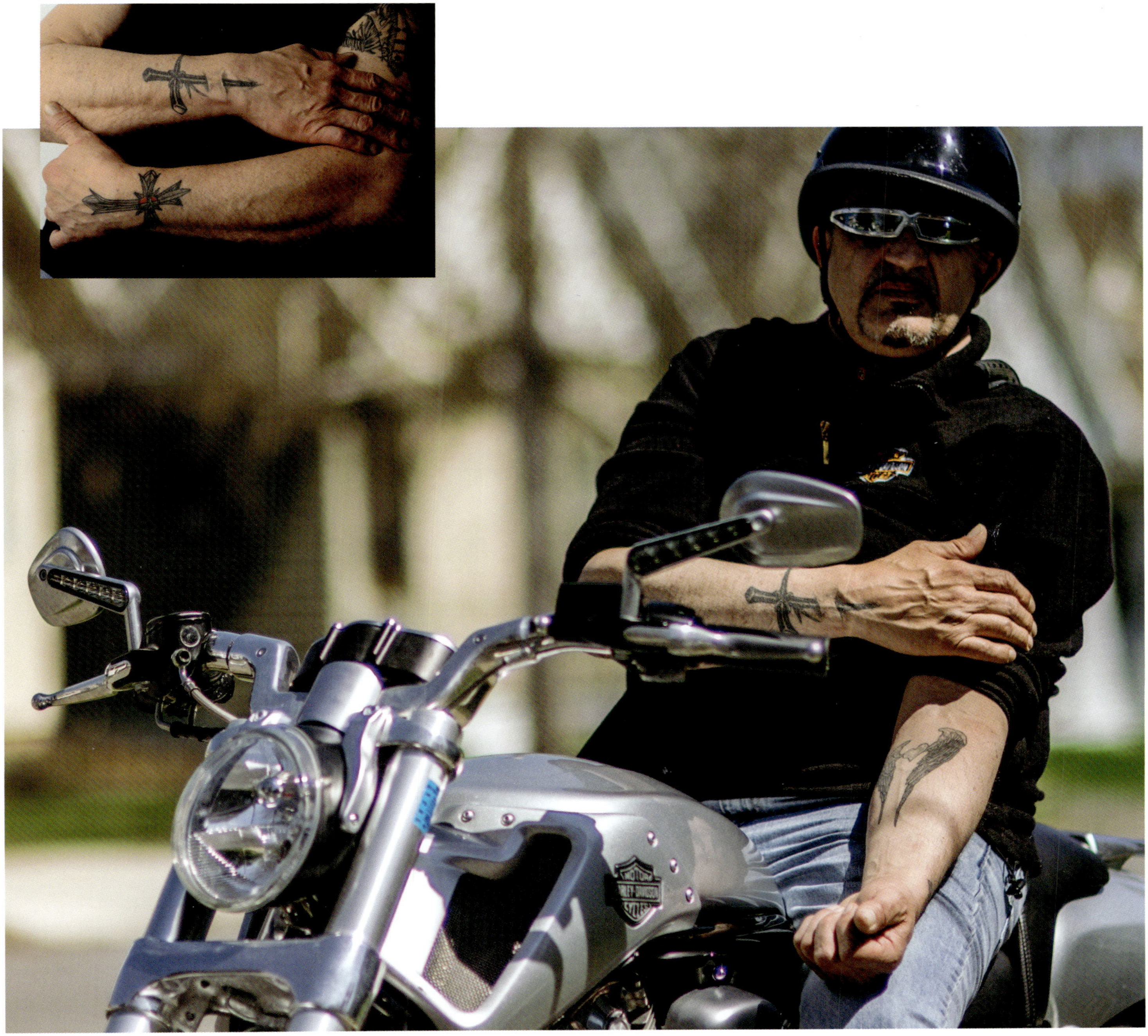

Joseph Dee

Photographs by David Lloyd and Ross J. Deater

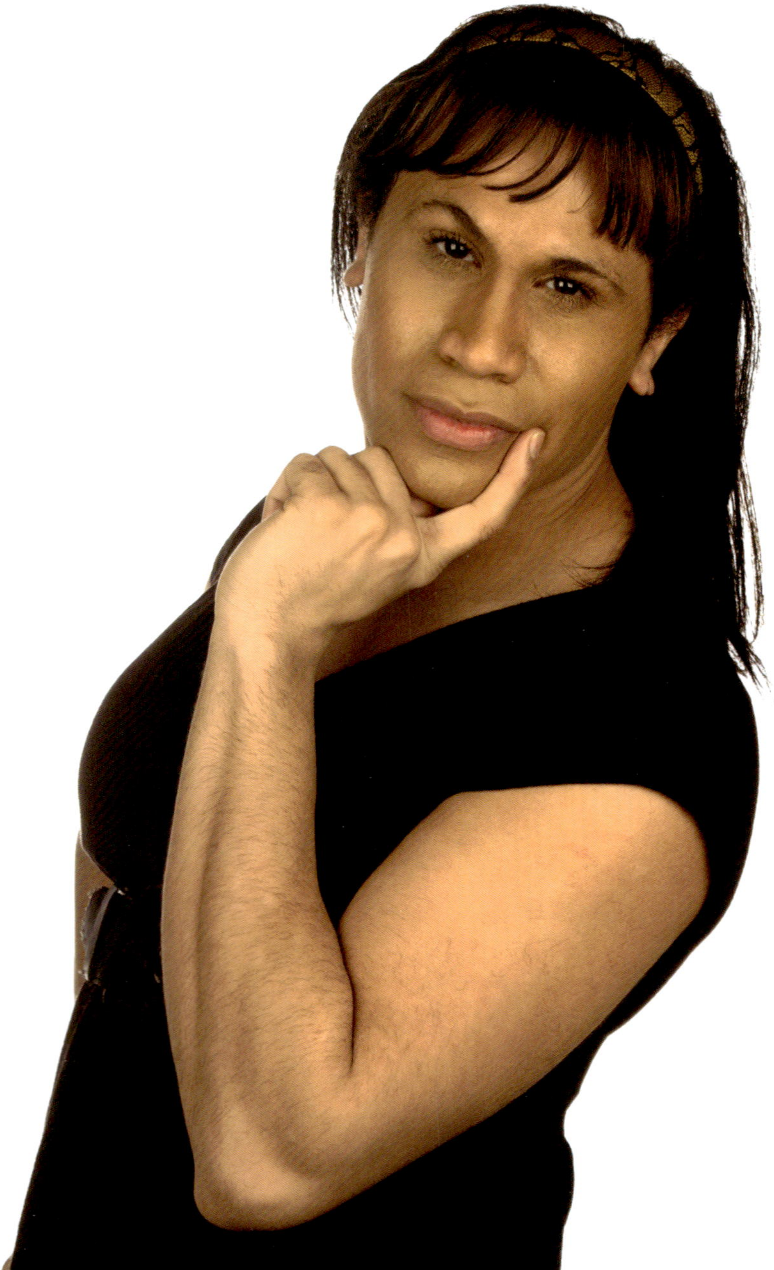

Michelle Rodriguez-Mendez
Photograph by Valerie Laubenheimer

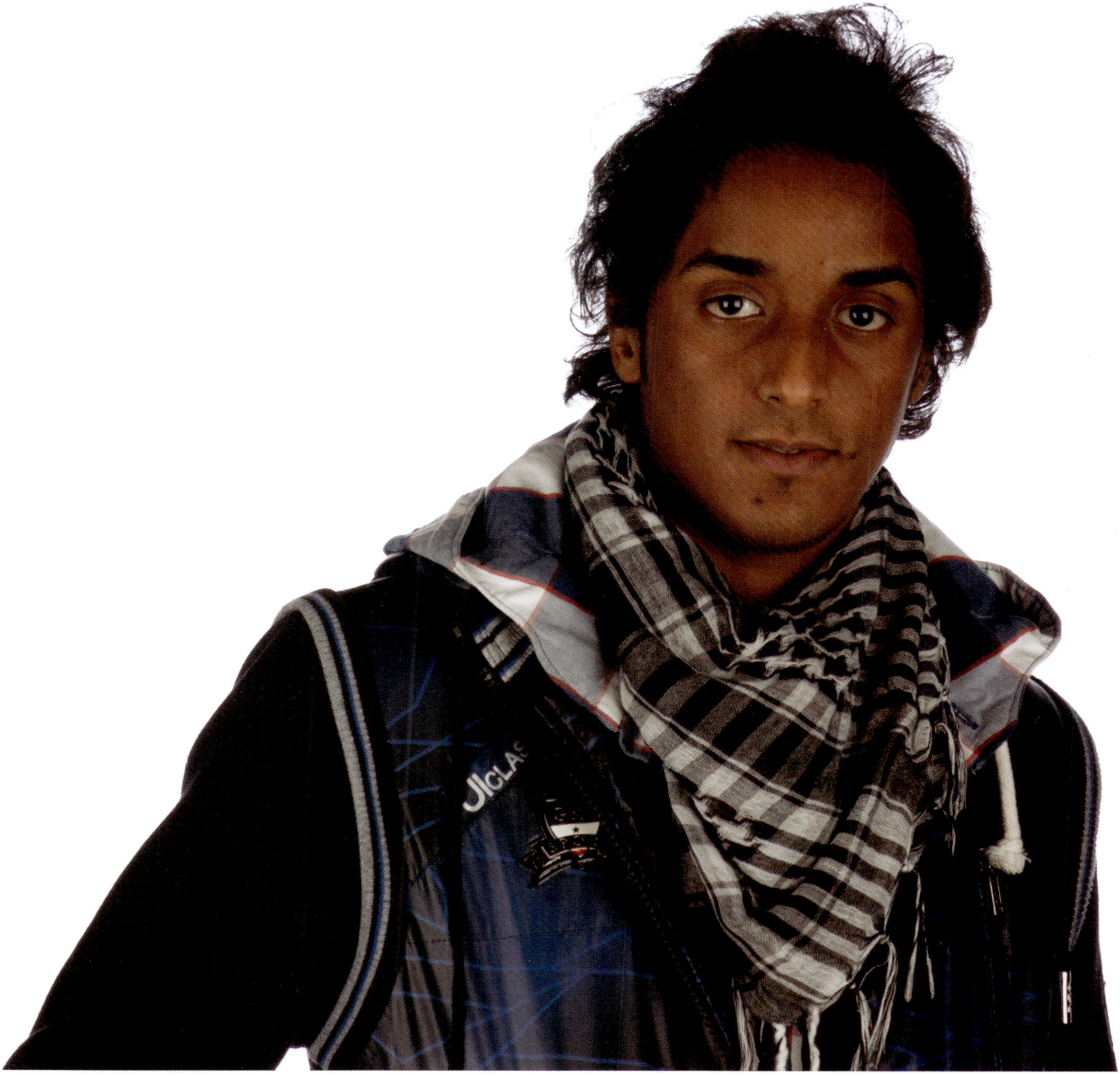

Mejeed Al-Dussary
Photograph by Robert Chapman

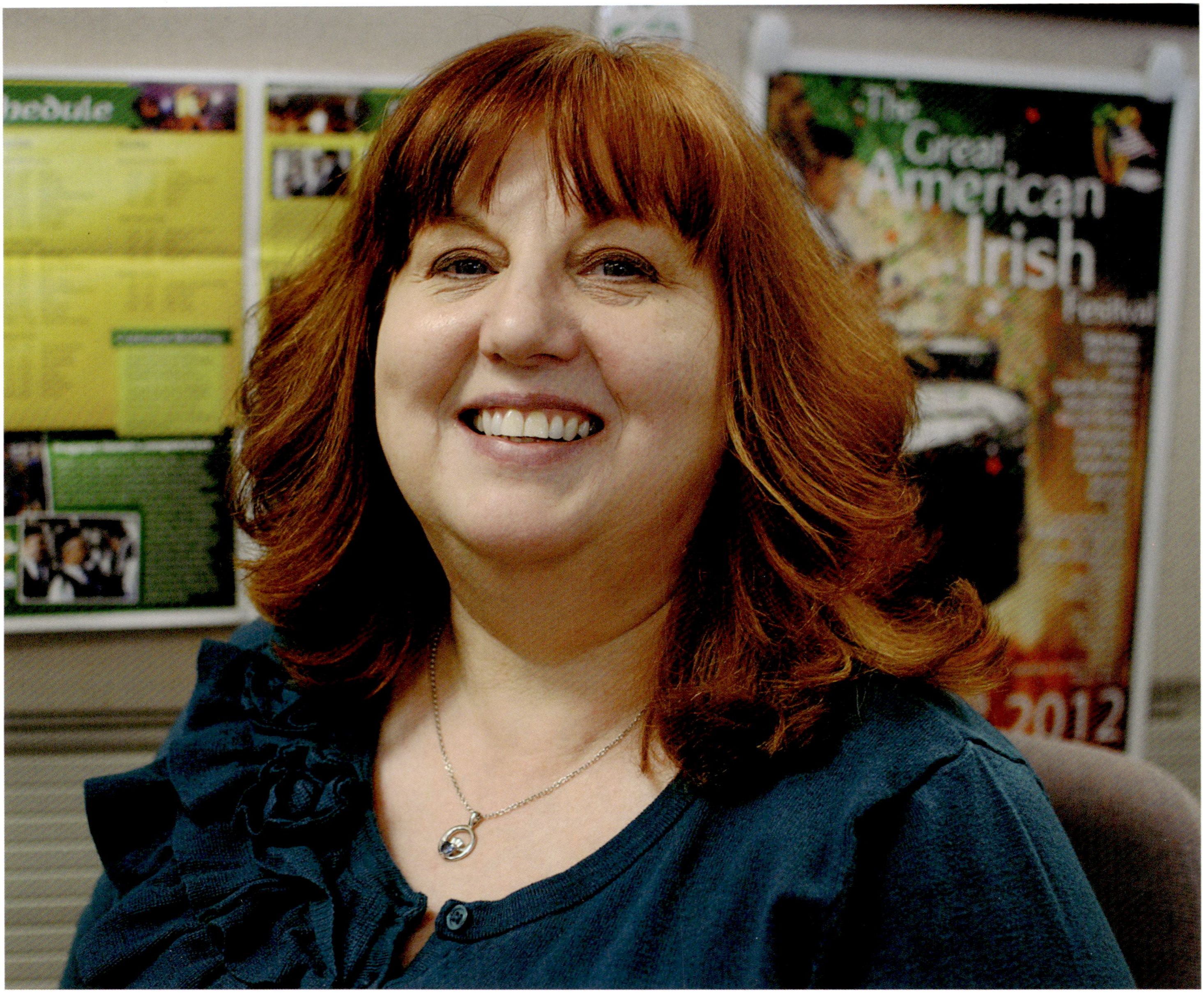

Kathryn Flanagan Barefoot
Photograph by Frederick F. Zang

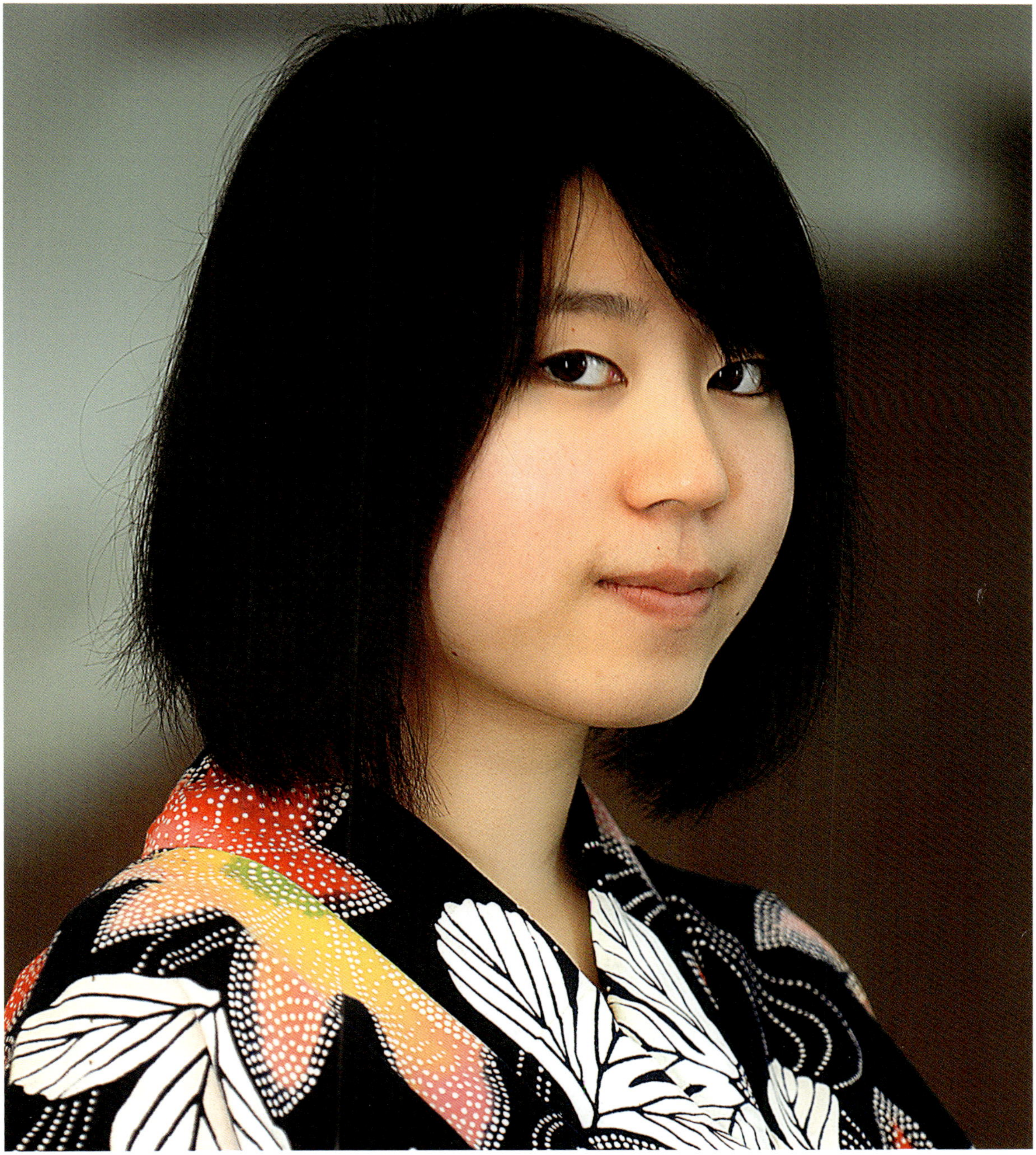

Tomomi Murayama
Photograph by Michael LaPolla

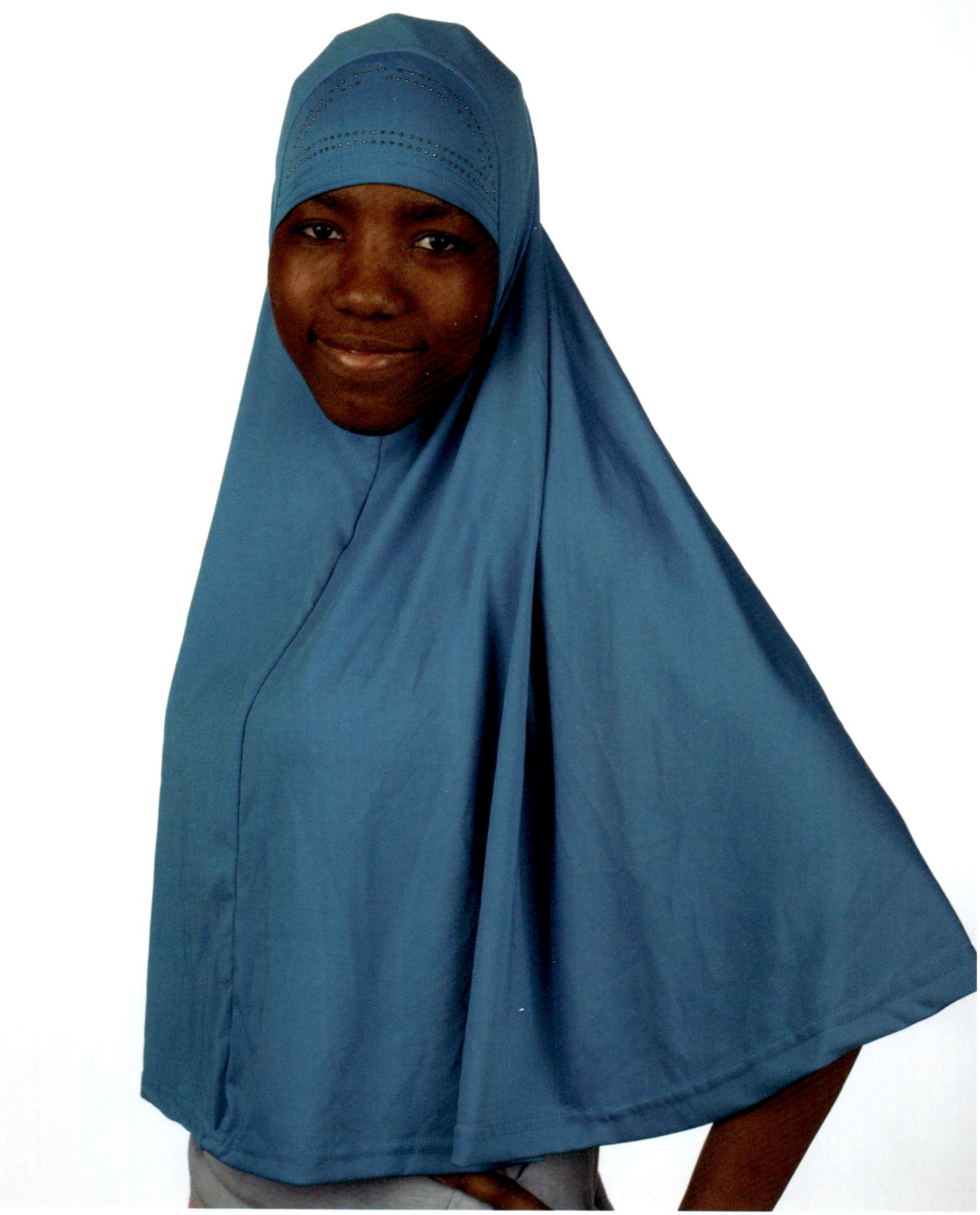

Mana Mudey
Photograph by Josh Szot

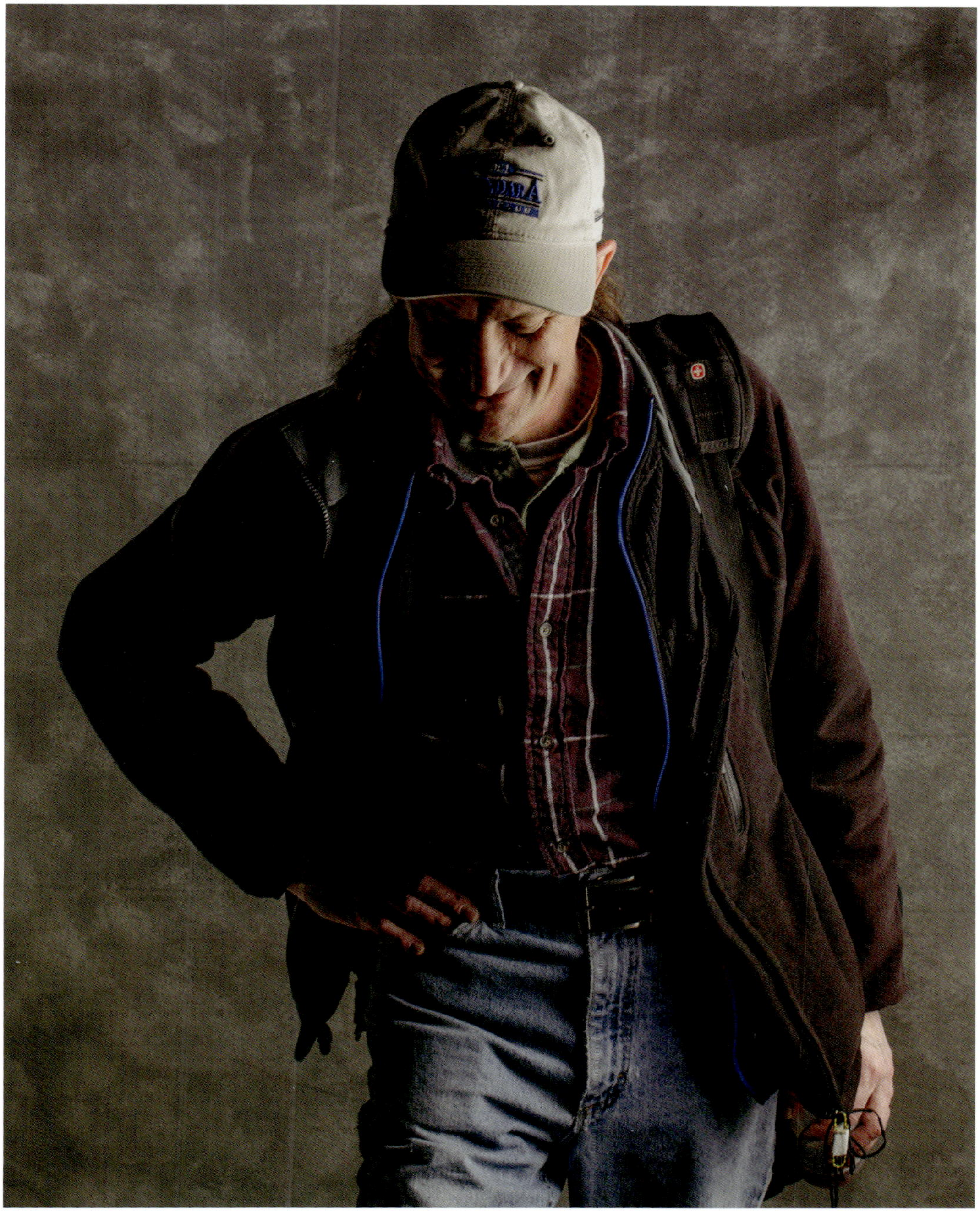

Douglas Hyldelund
Photograph by Kayla Emery

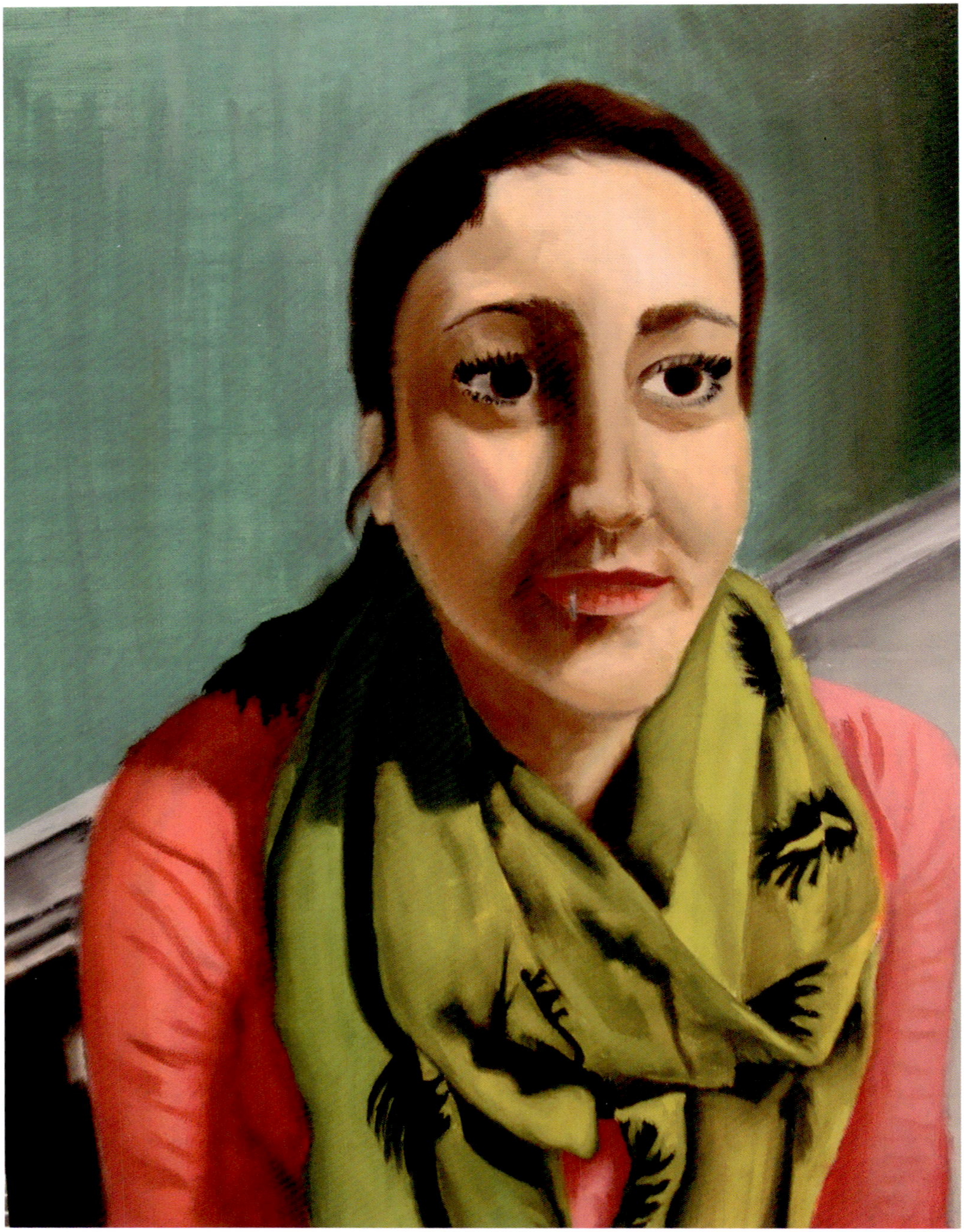

Angela Munyon
Painting by Anastasia Docherty

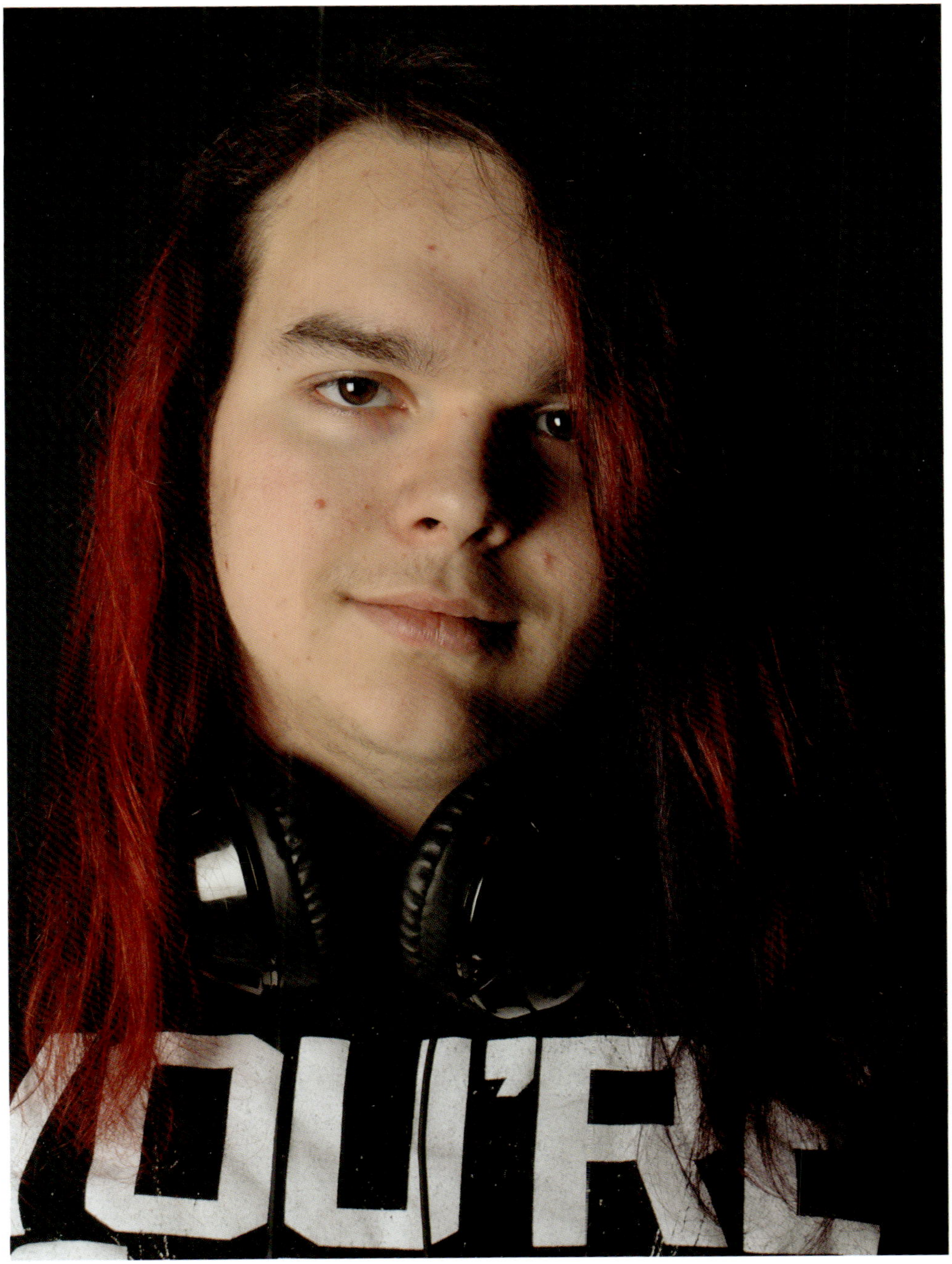

Trevor Anderson
Photograph by Eden Richardson

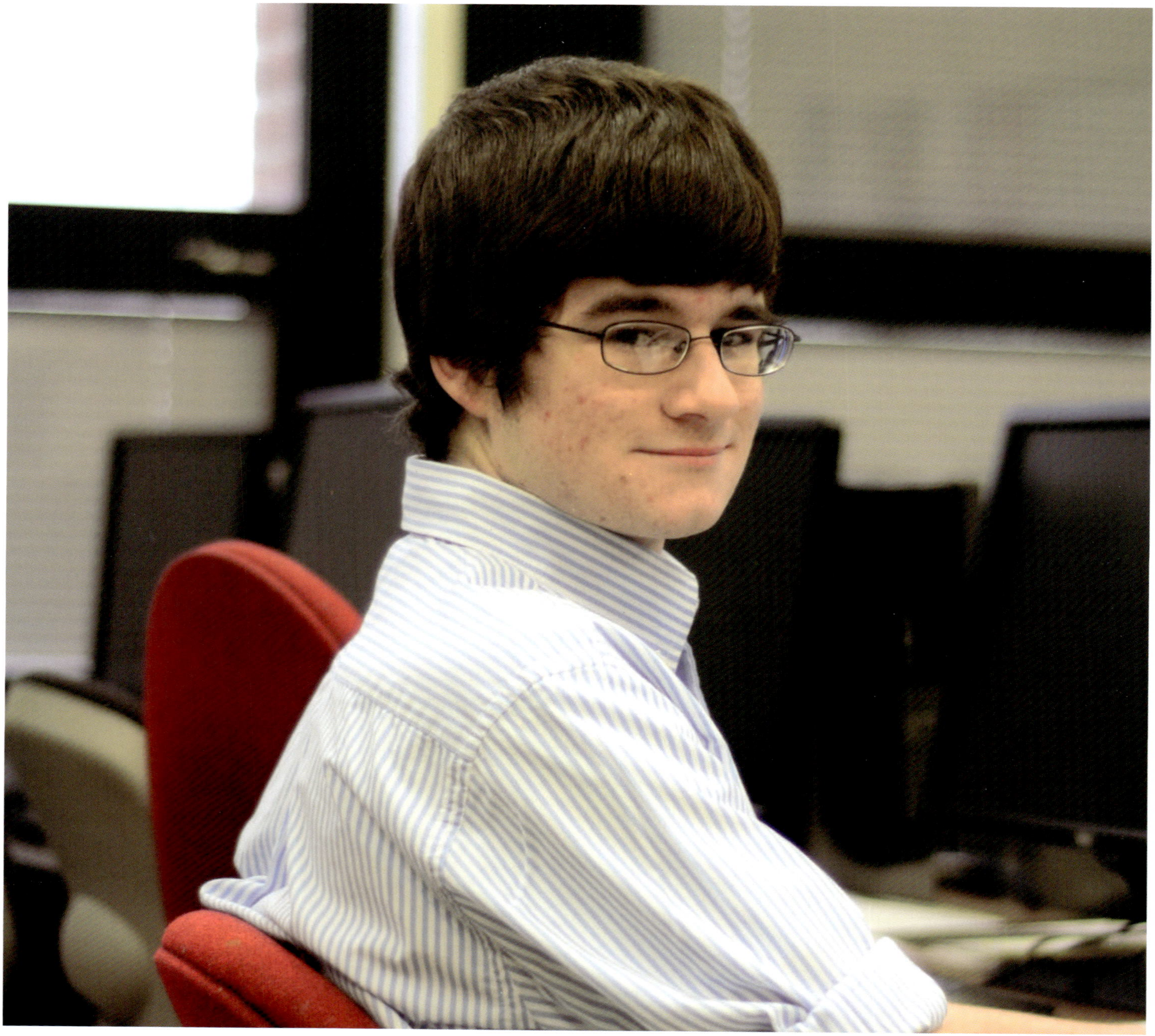

Tyler Humphreys
Photograph by David Lloyd

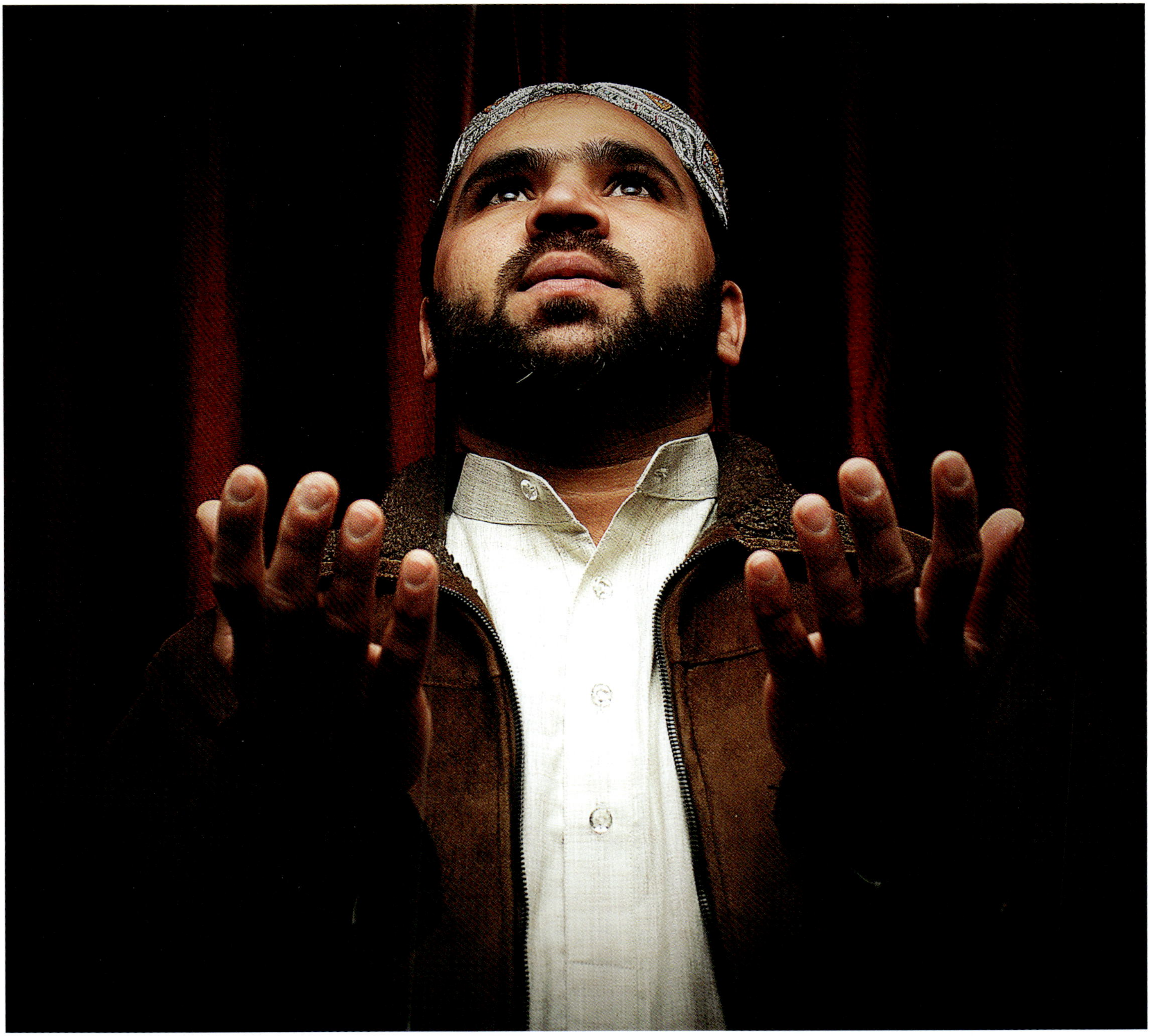

Shafqet Ali
Photograph by Michael LaPolla

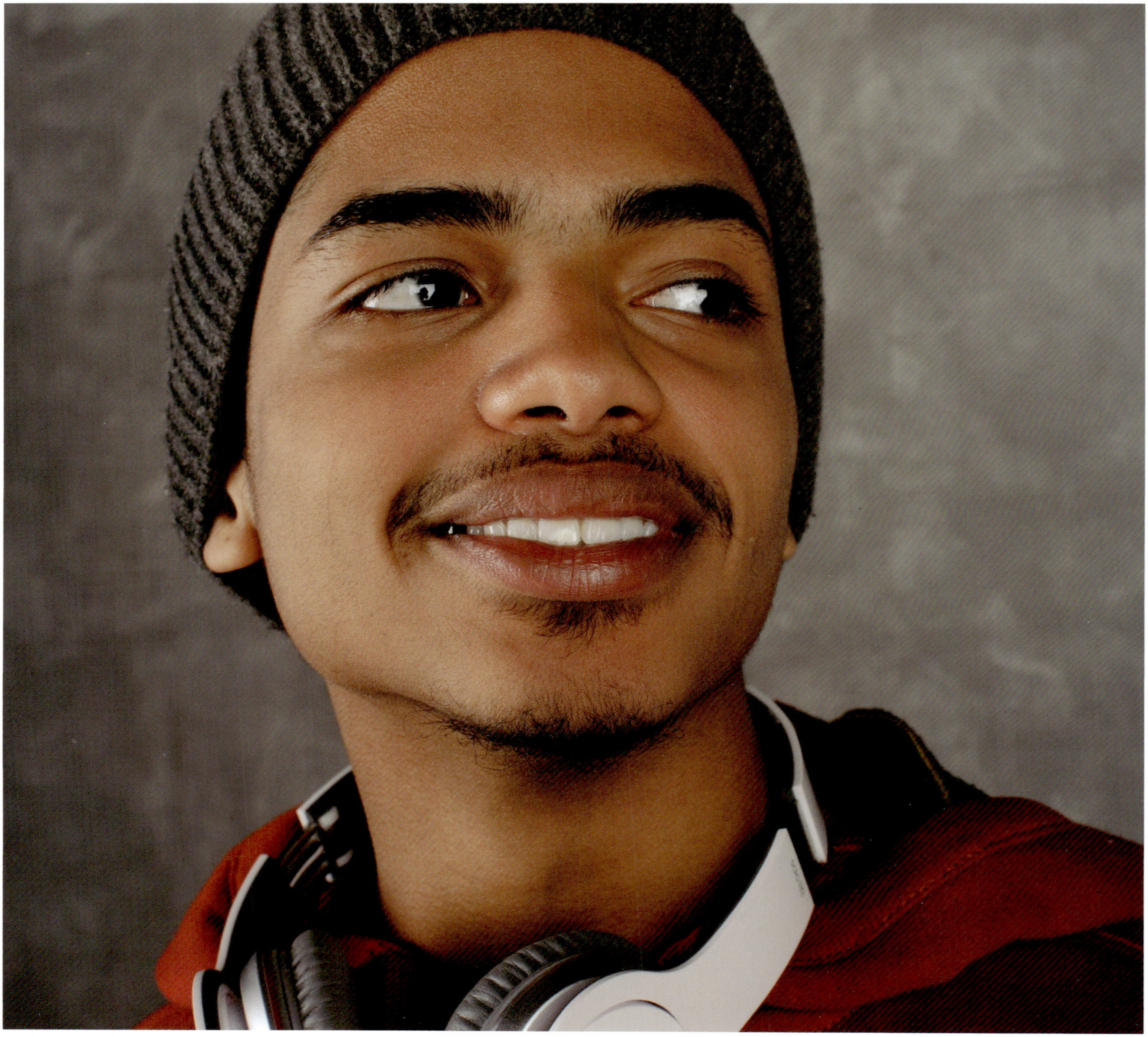

Yohevian CHiiKi Polanco
Photograph by Frederick F. Zang

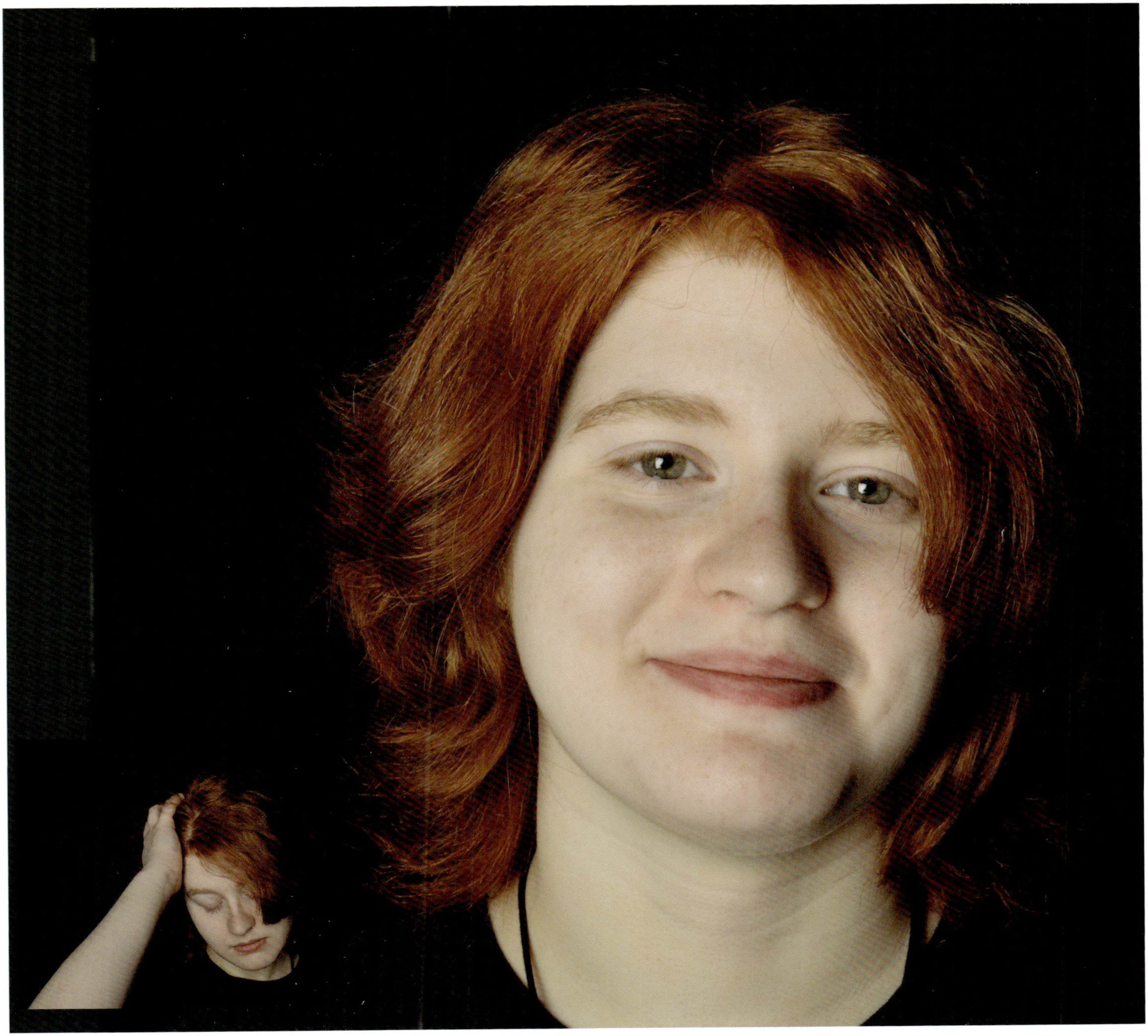

Danielle Brownell

Photographs by Aaron Deming

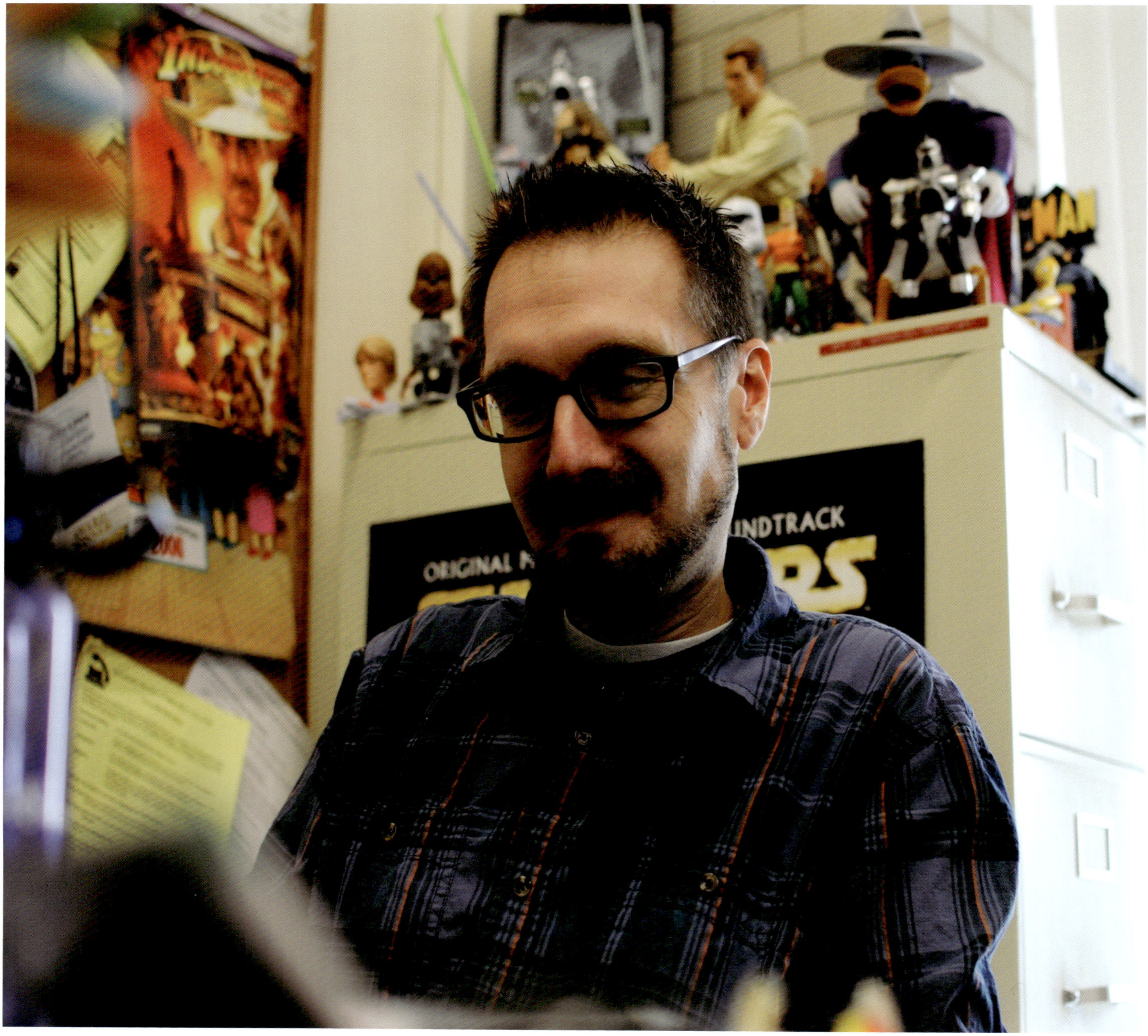

Kyle A. Lince
Photograph by Frederick F. Zang

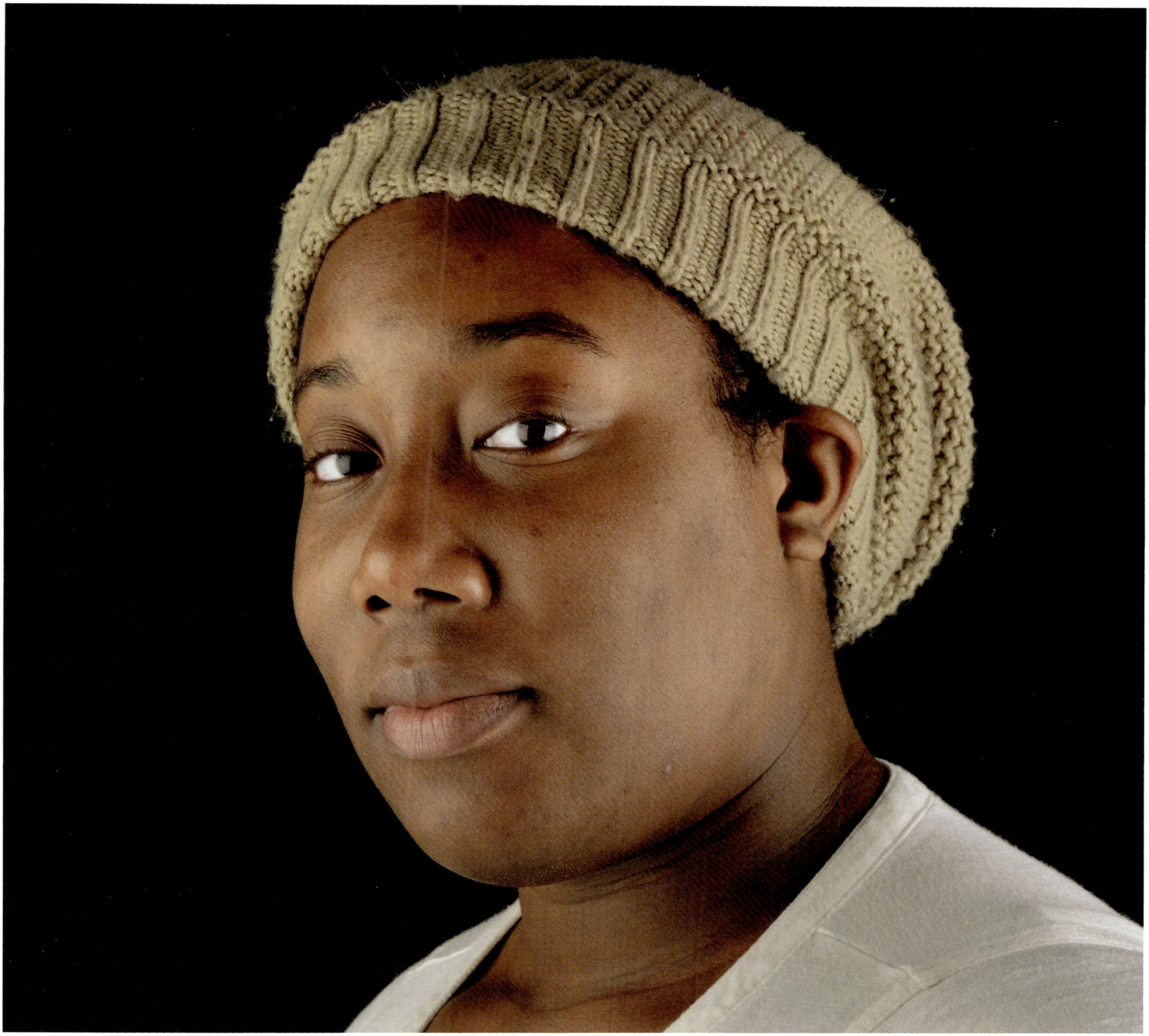

Eden Richardson
Photograph by Joshua F. Pitcher

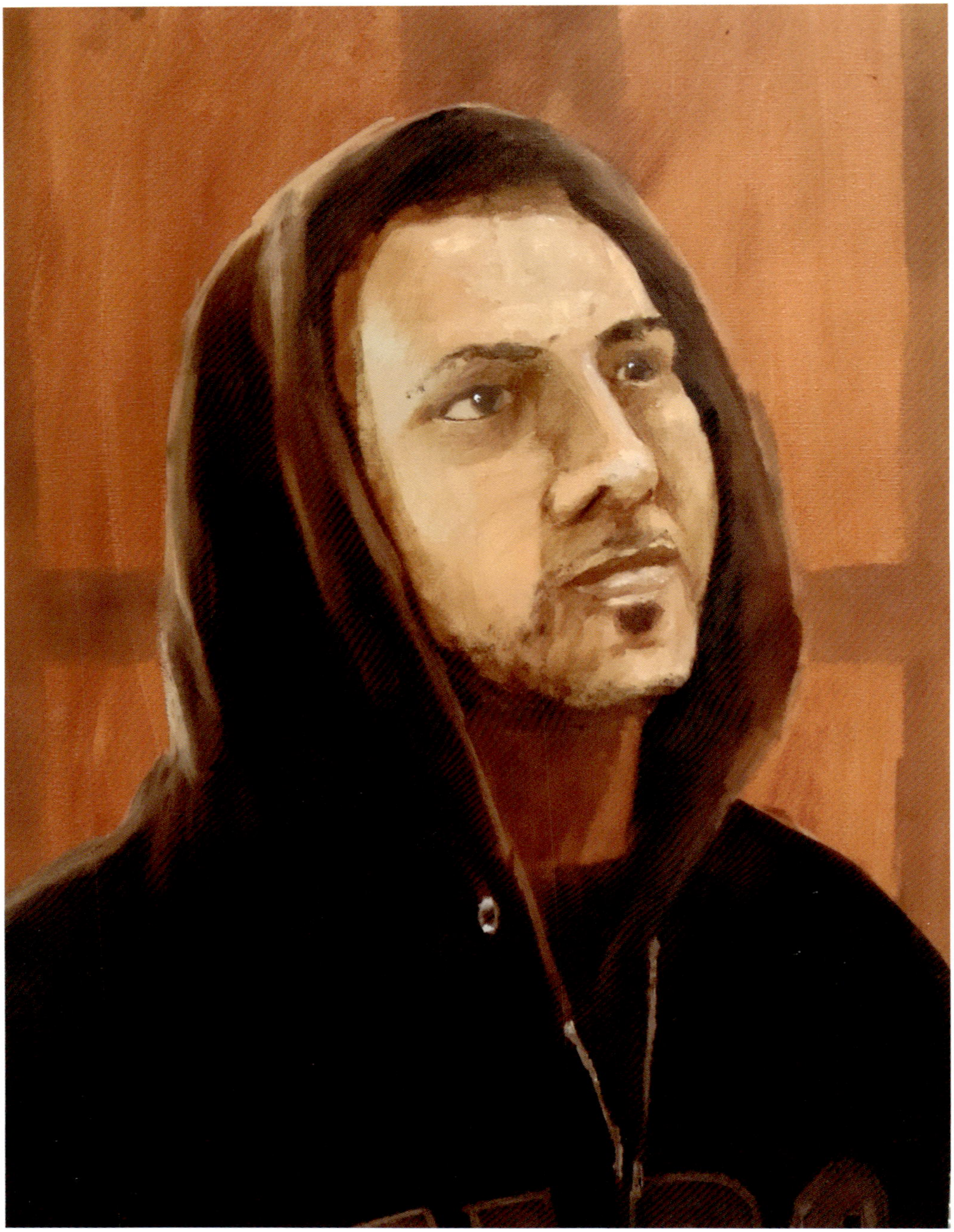

Seval Rahic
Painting by Rebekah Yeater

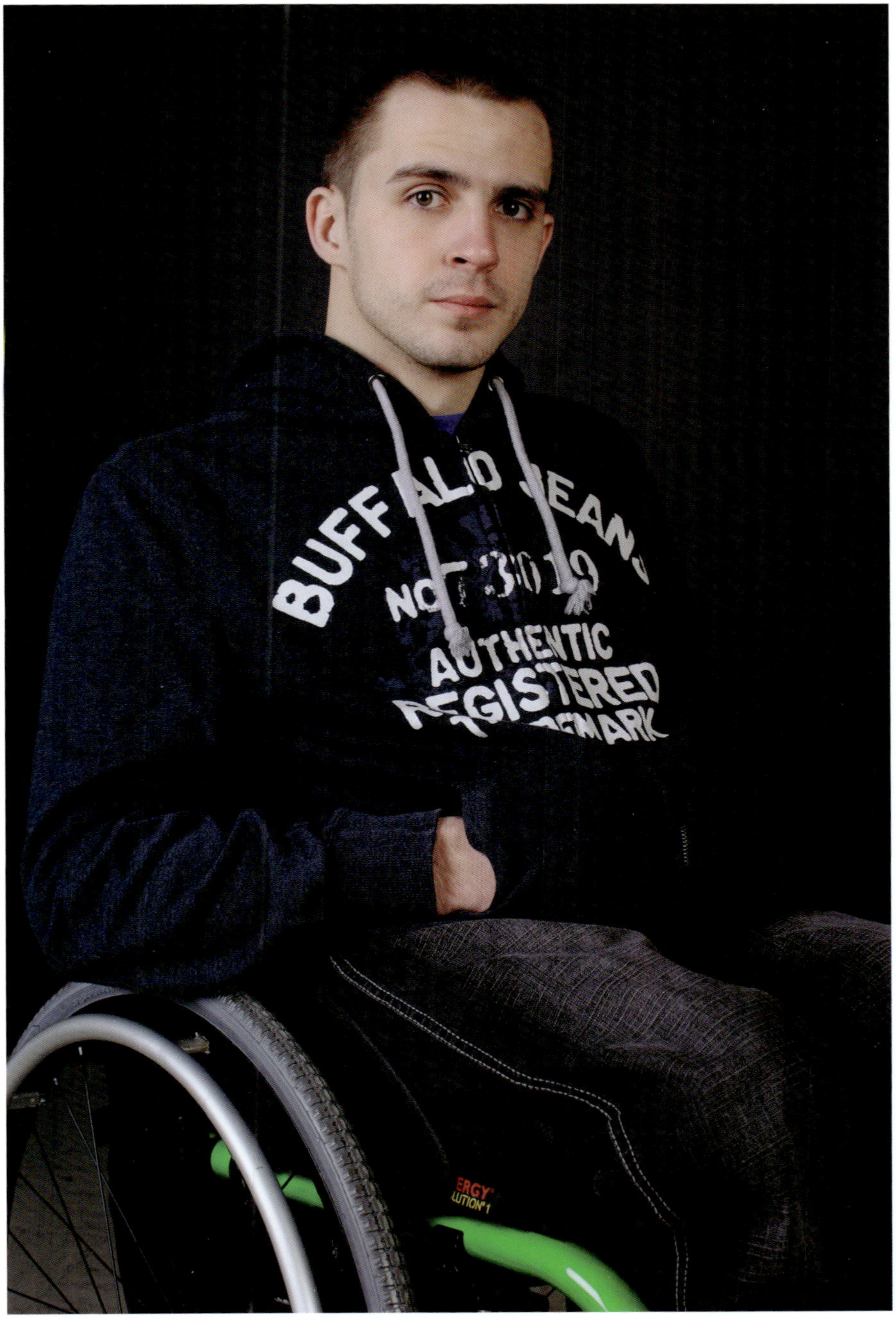

Hermin Garic
Photograph by Frederick F. Zang

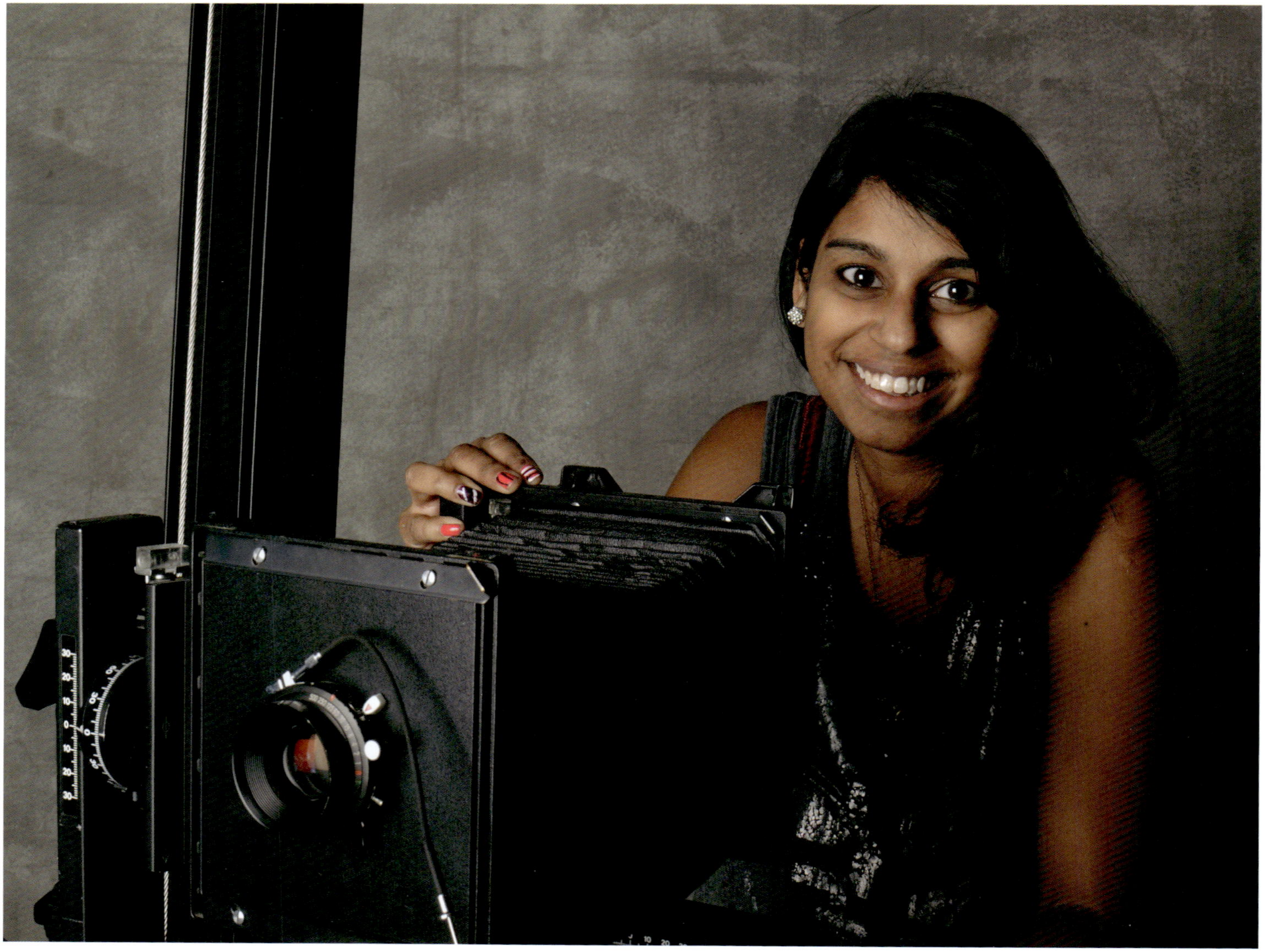

Rebekah Soule
Photograph by Aaron Deming

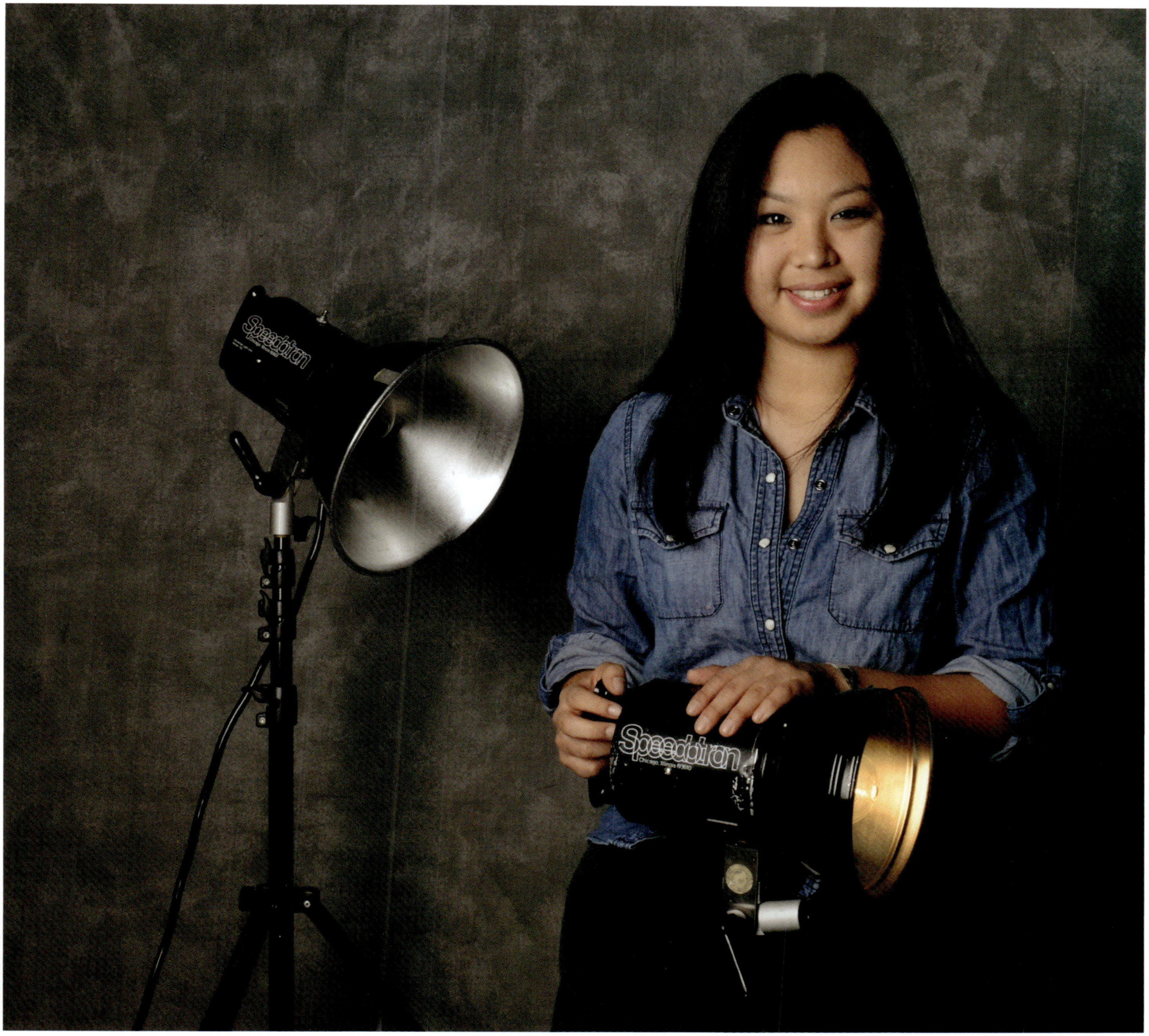

Marsha Chamberlin
Photograph by Aaron Deming

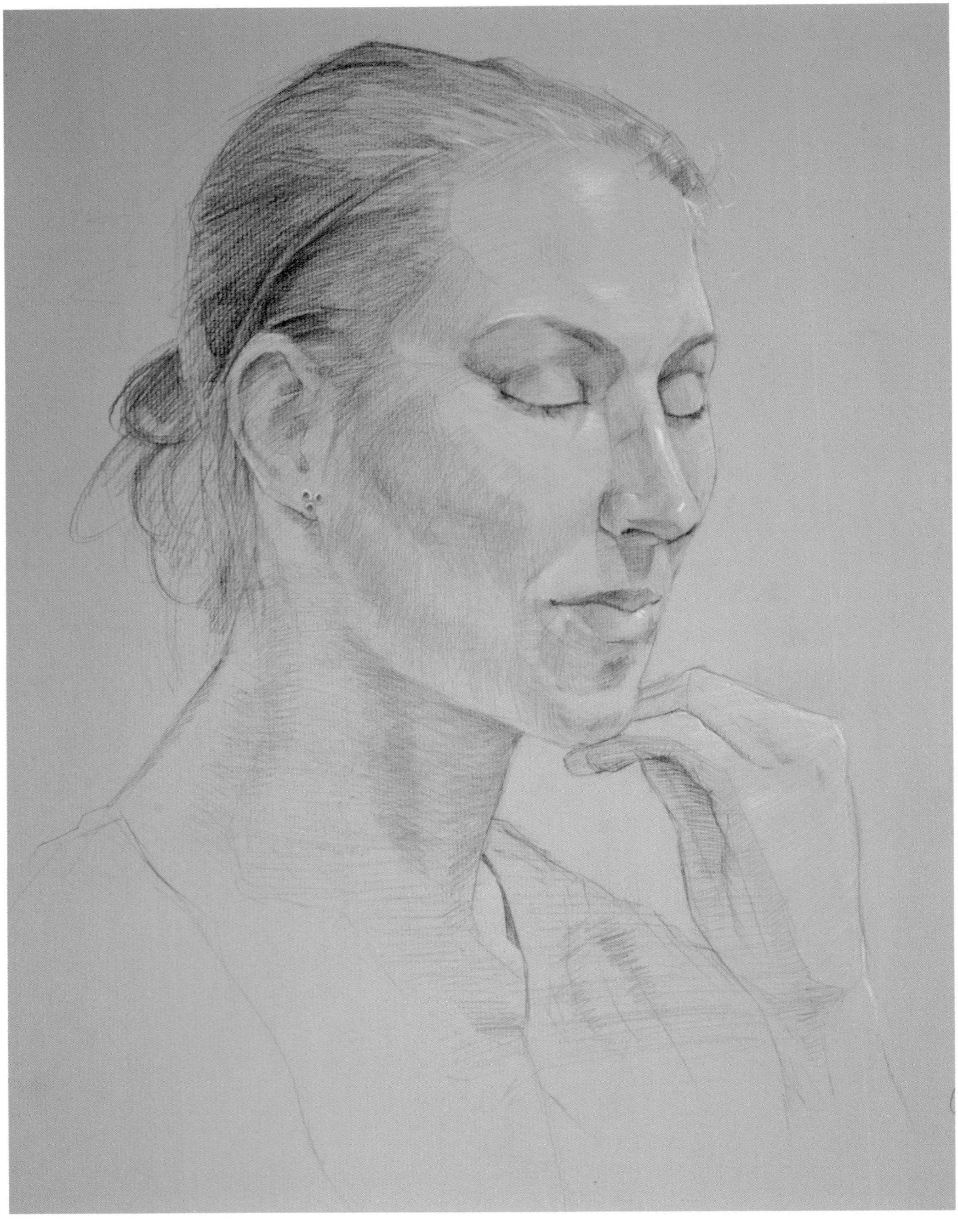

Liz Easton
Drawing by Marcus Foley

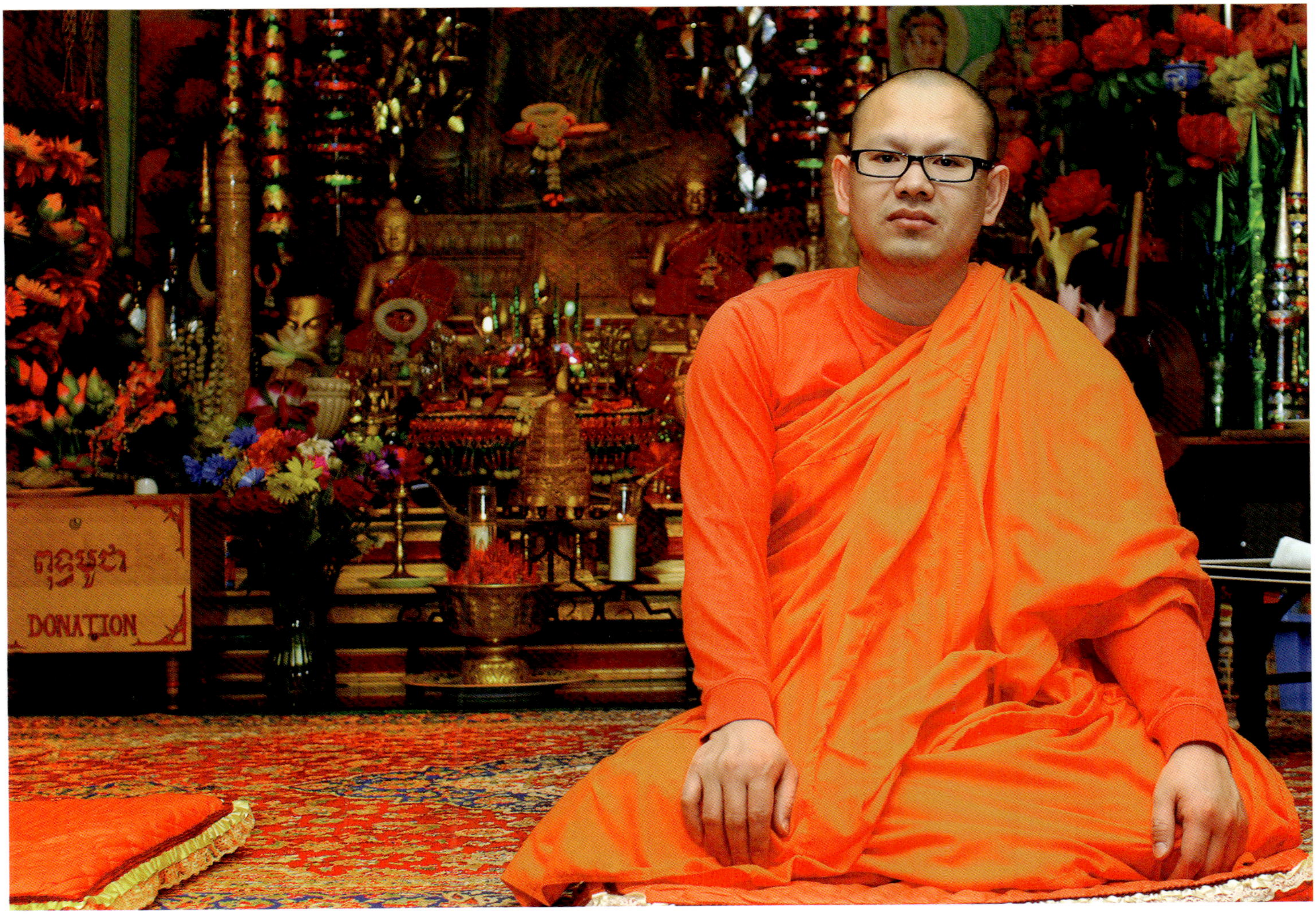

Sokhom Teng
Photograph by Terry Burton

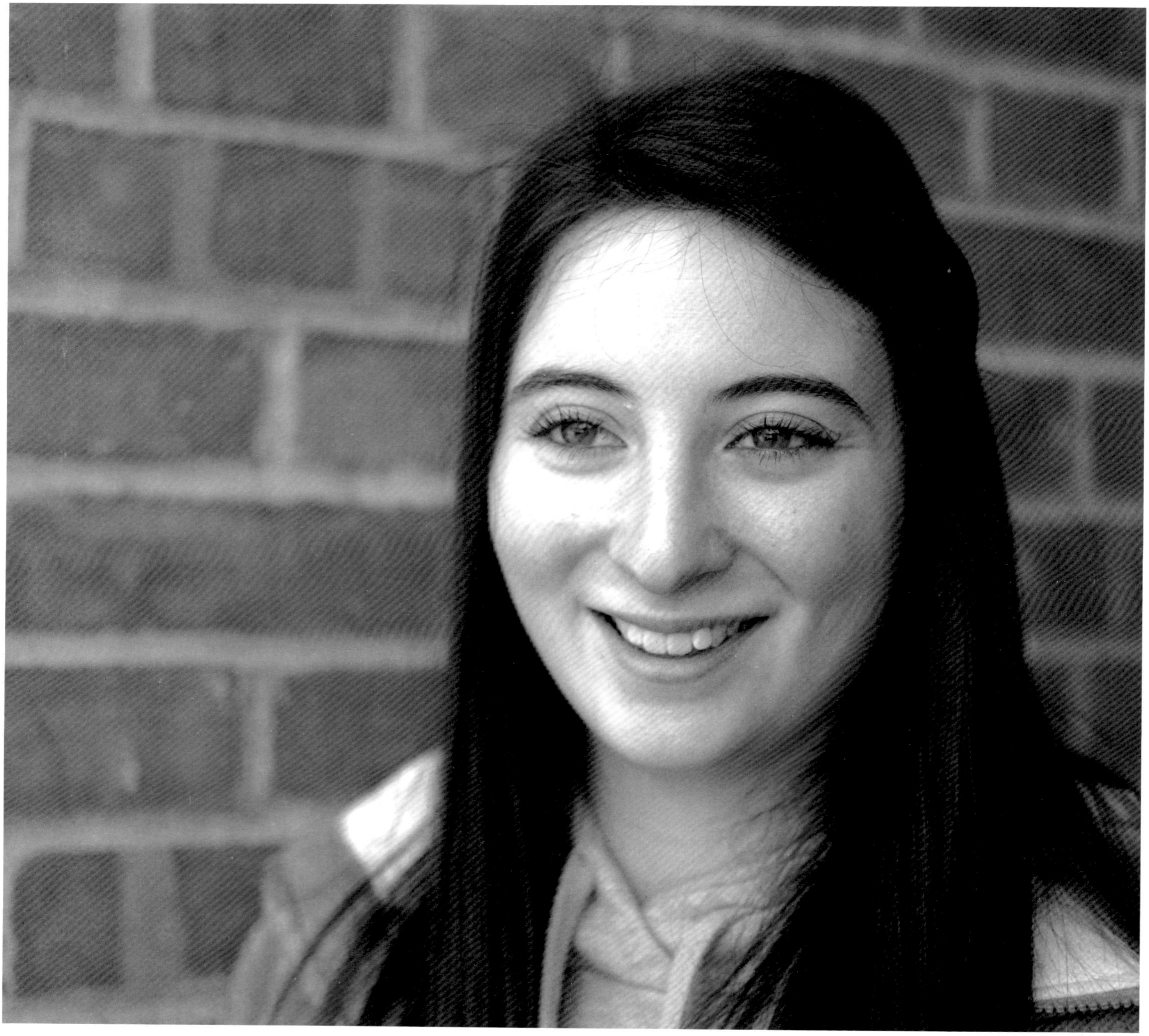

Willow Simmons-Nackley
Photograph by Joshua F. Pitcher

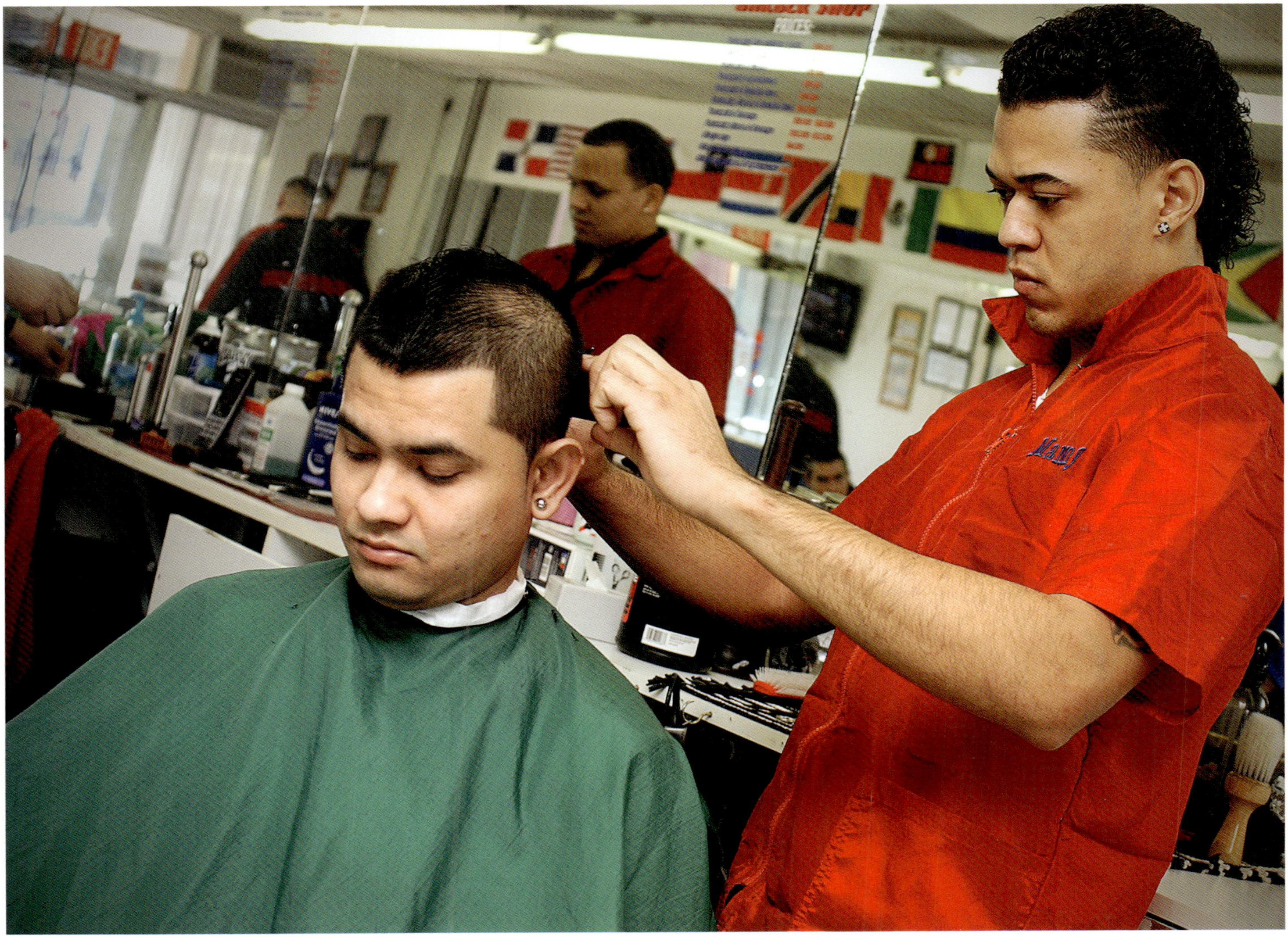

Roberto Paredes
Photograph by Michael LaPolla

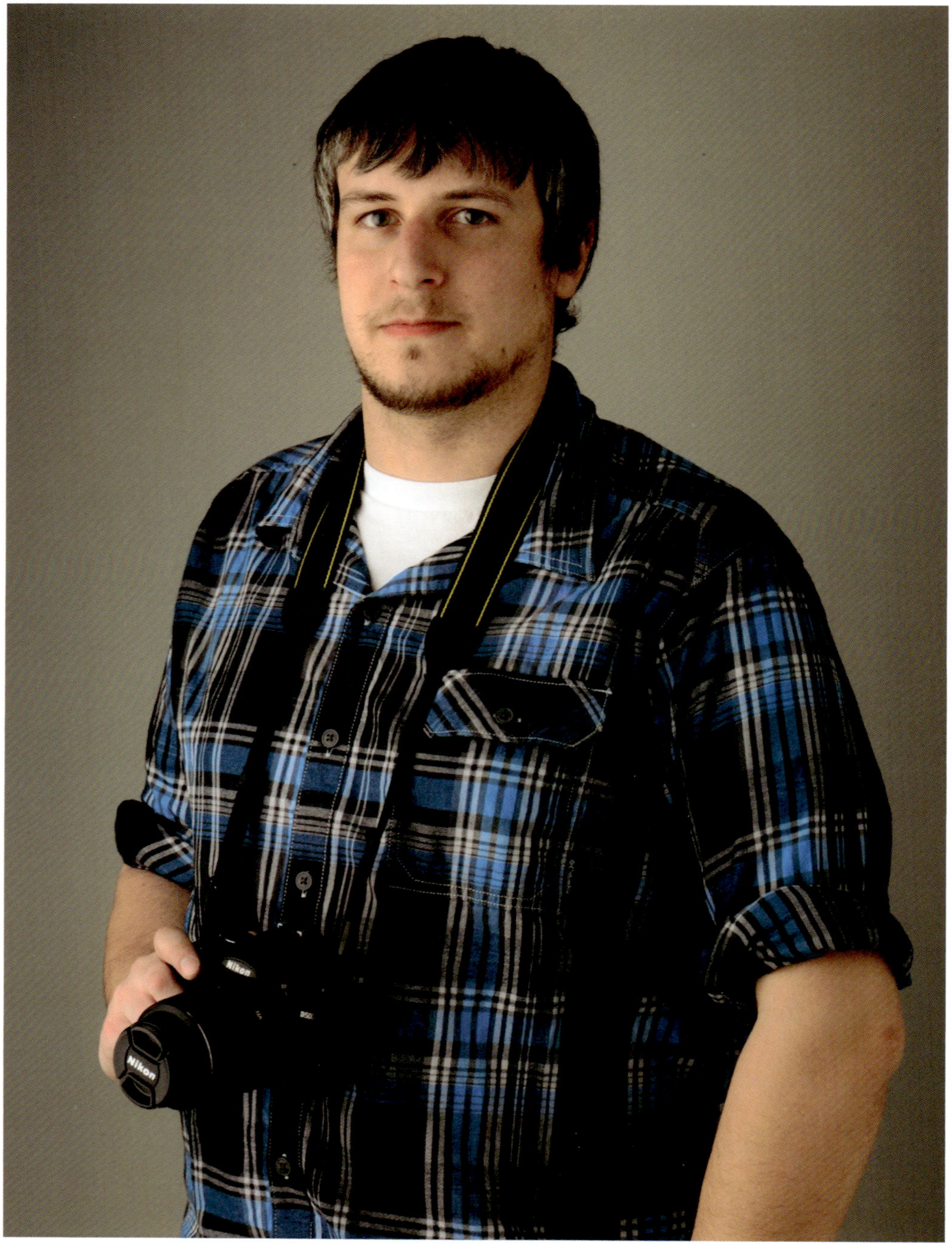

Ron Jones
Photograph by David Lloyd

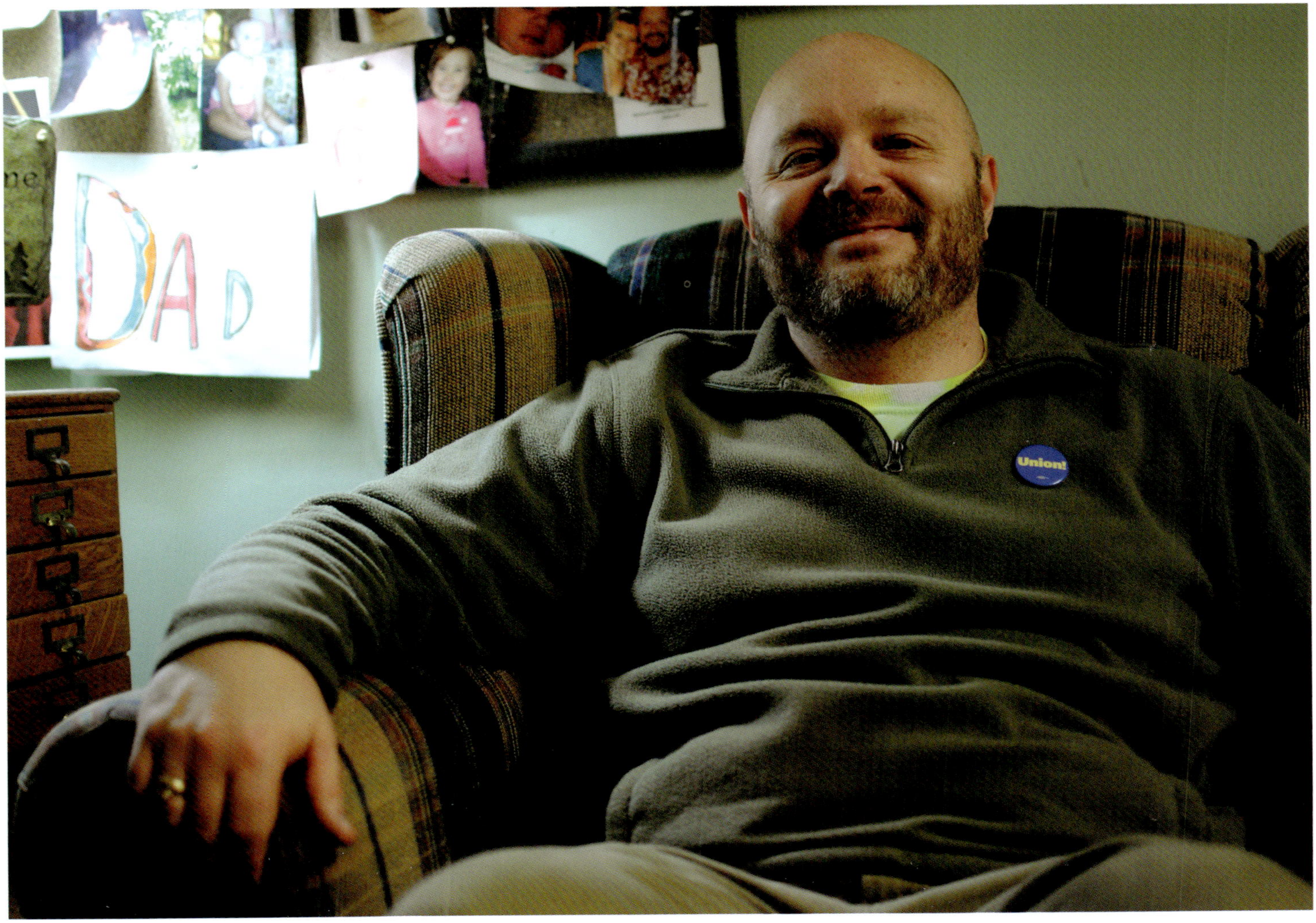

Dawson Paul McDermott
Photograph by Frederick F. Zang

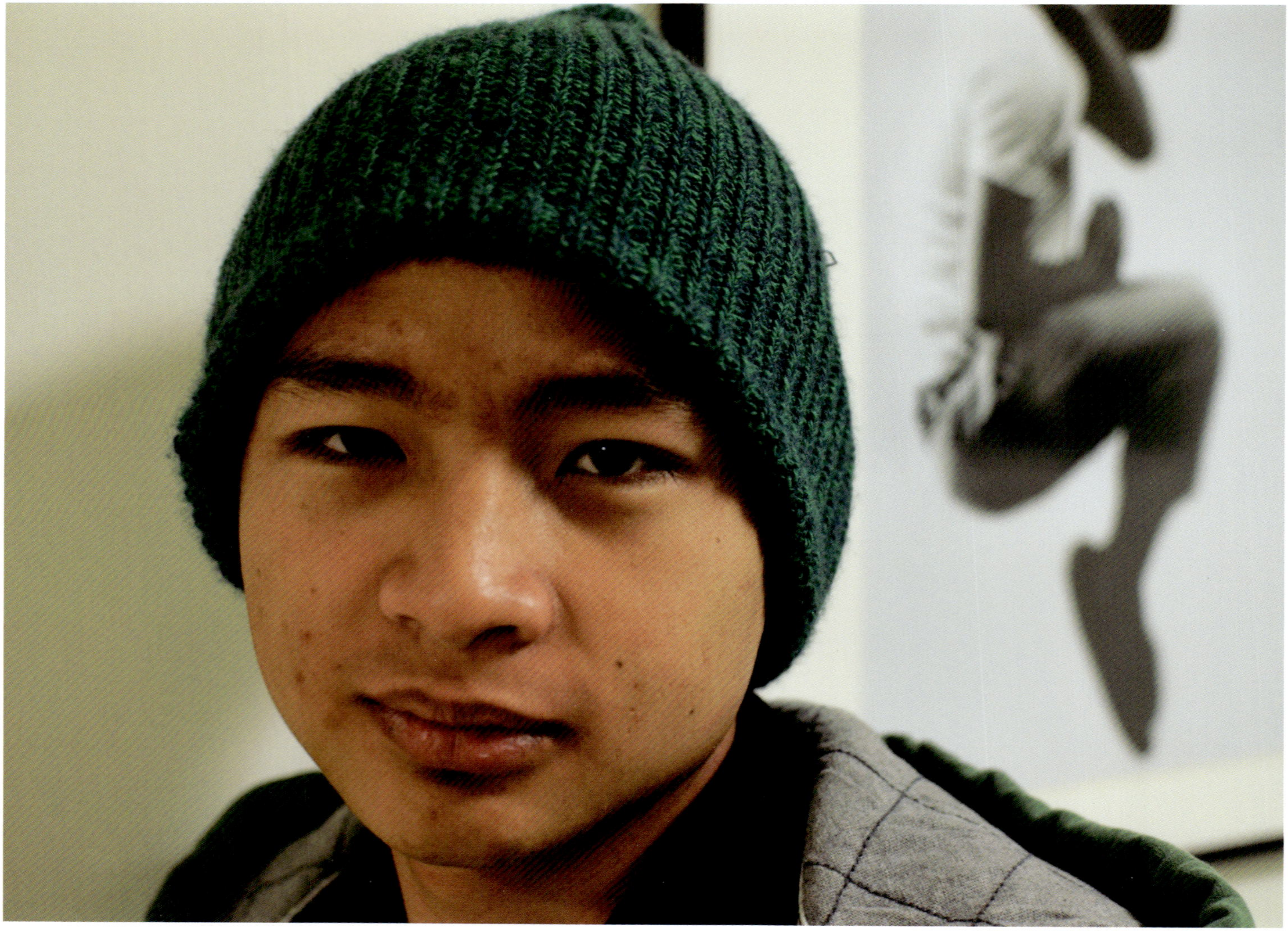

Journey Gyi
Photograph by Aaron Deming

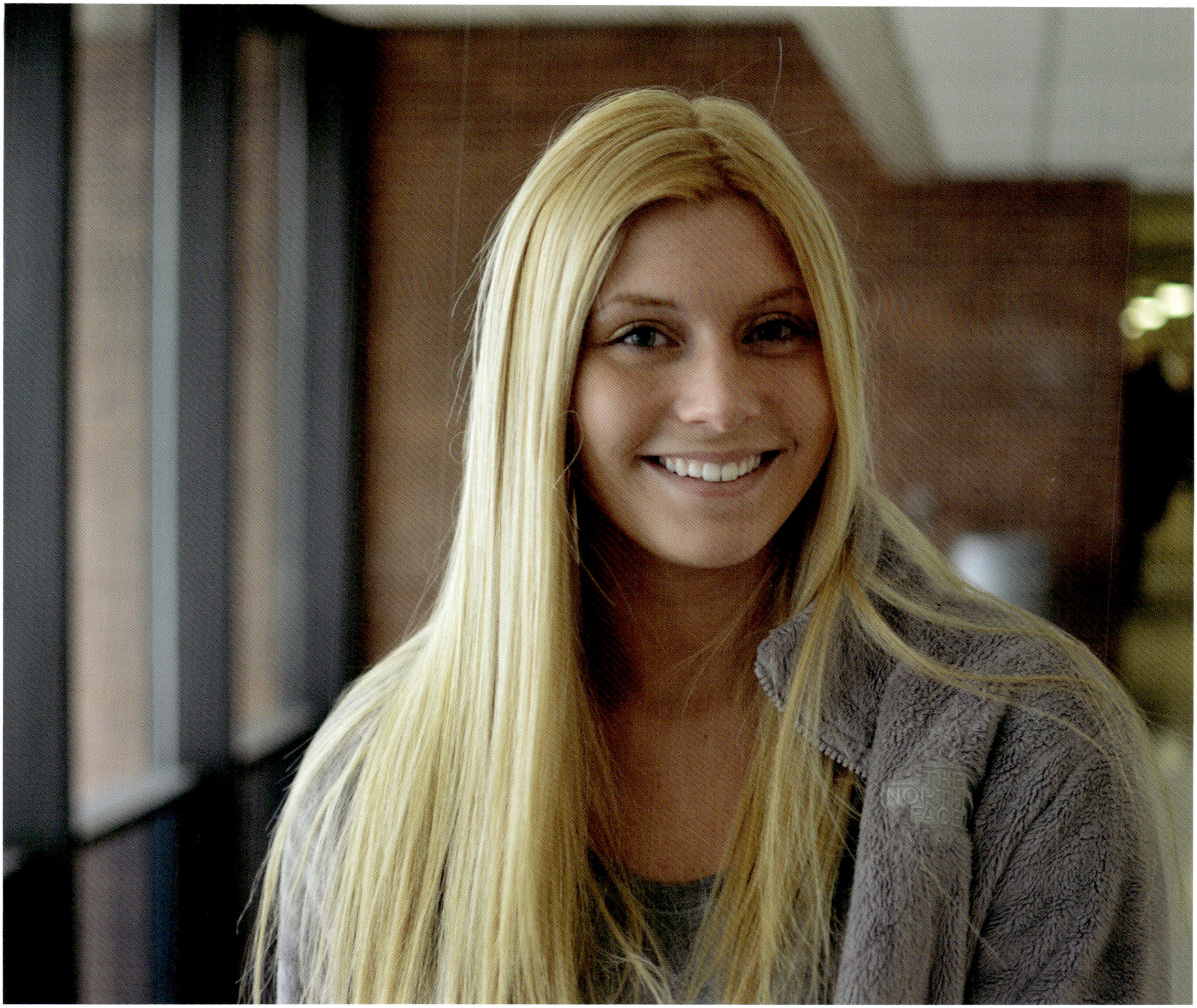

Haleigh Welch
Photograph by Joshua F. Pitcher

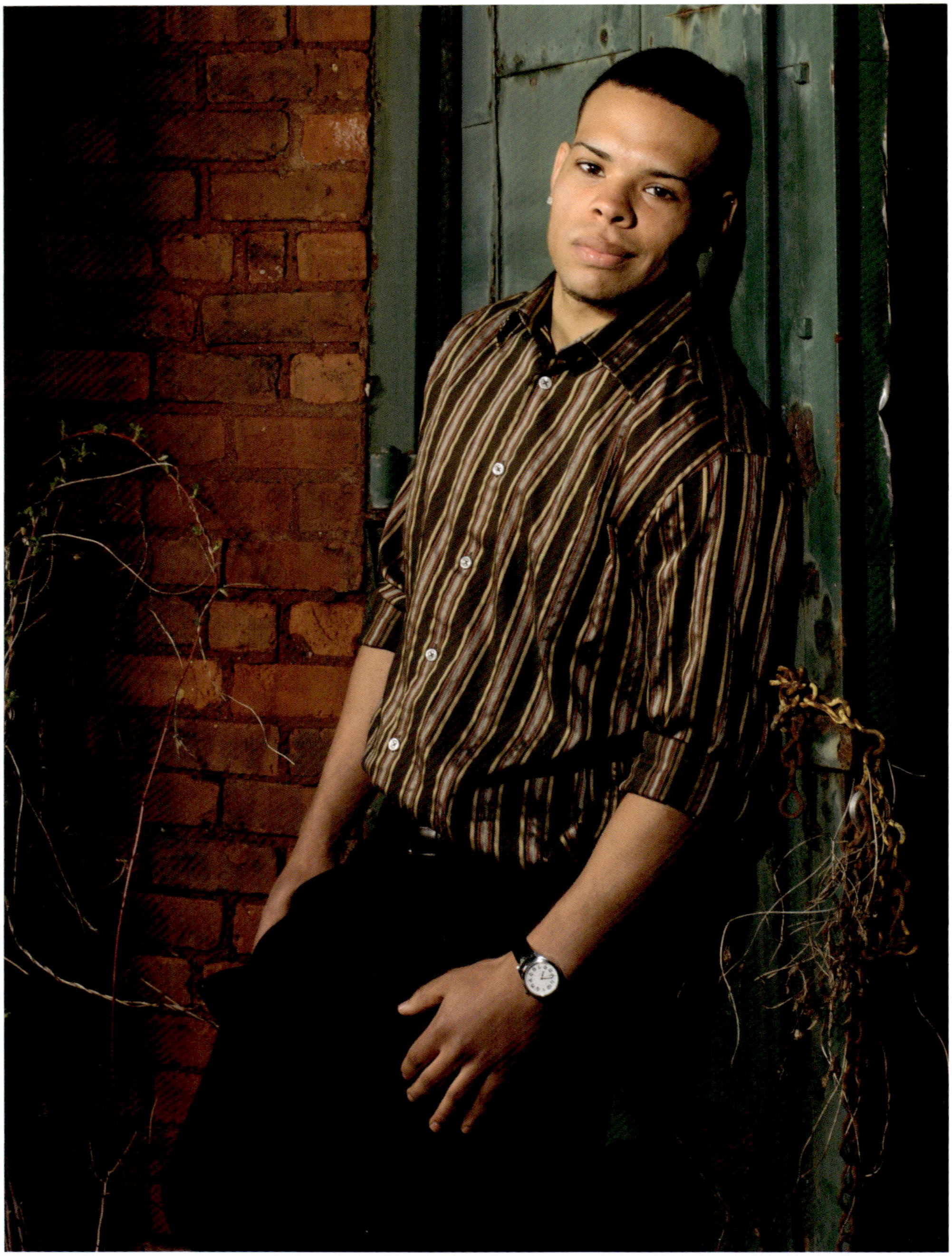

Kelvin Lizardo
Photograph by Indhira Grullon

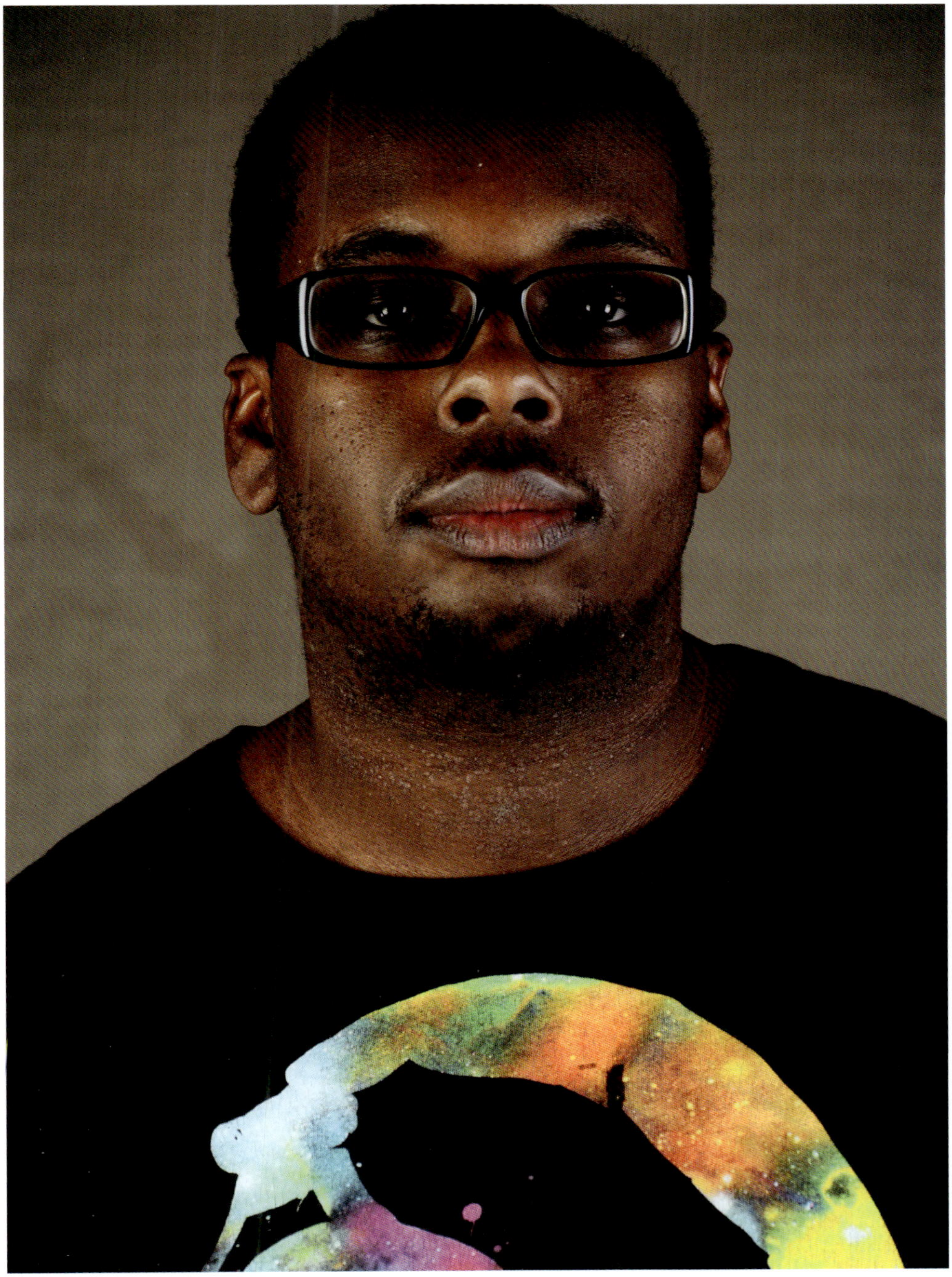

Kevin Q. Curtis
Photograph by Frederick F. Zang

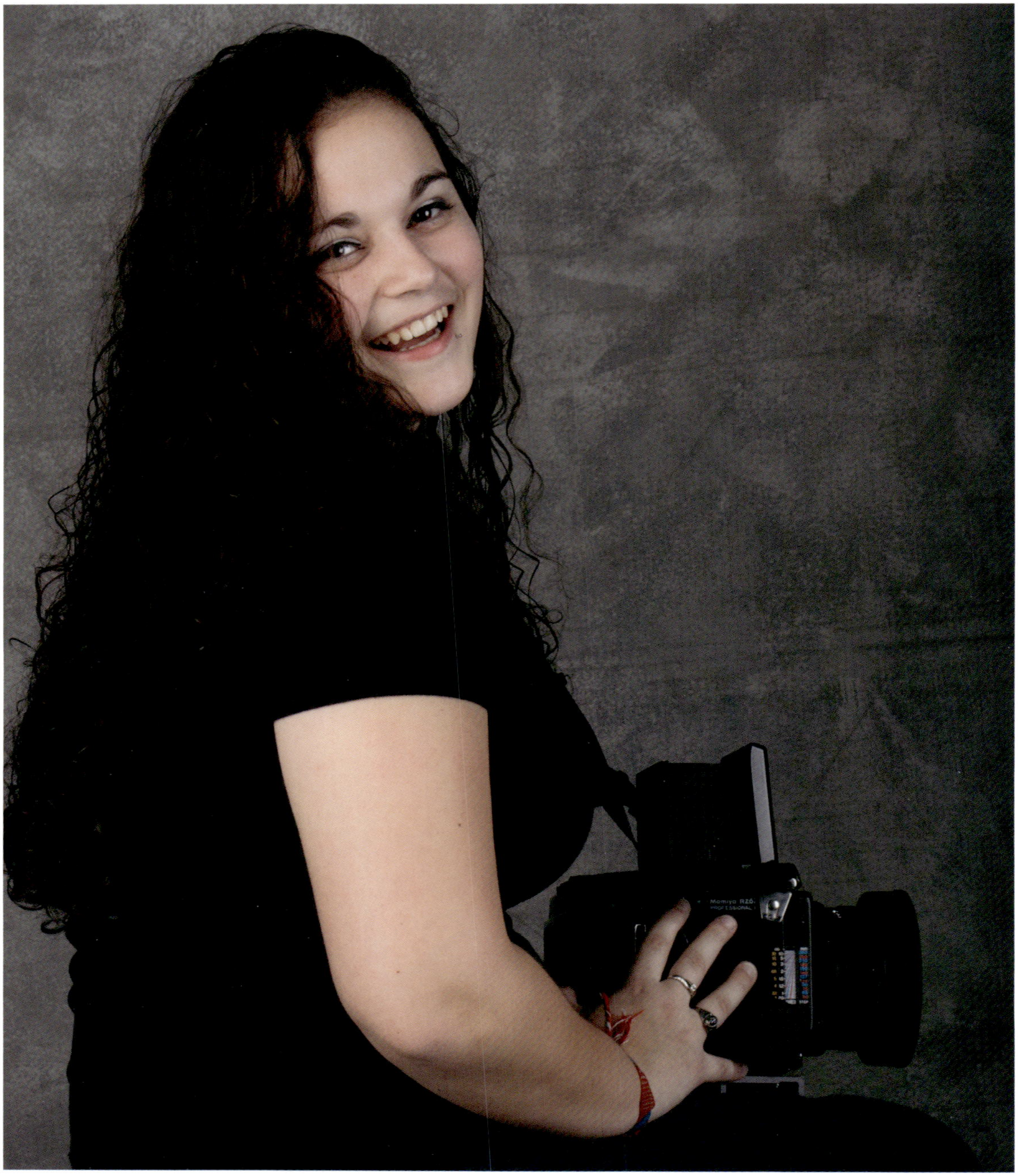

Kerisha Puerile
Photograph by Ron Jones

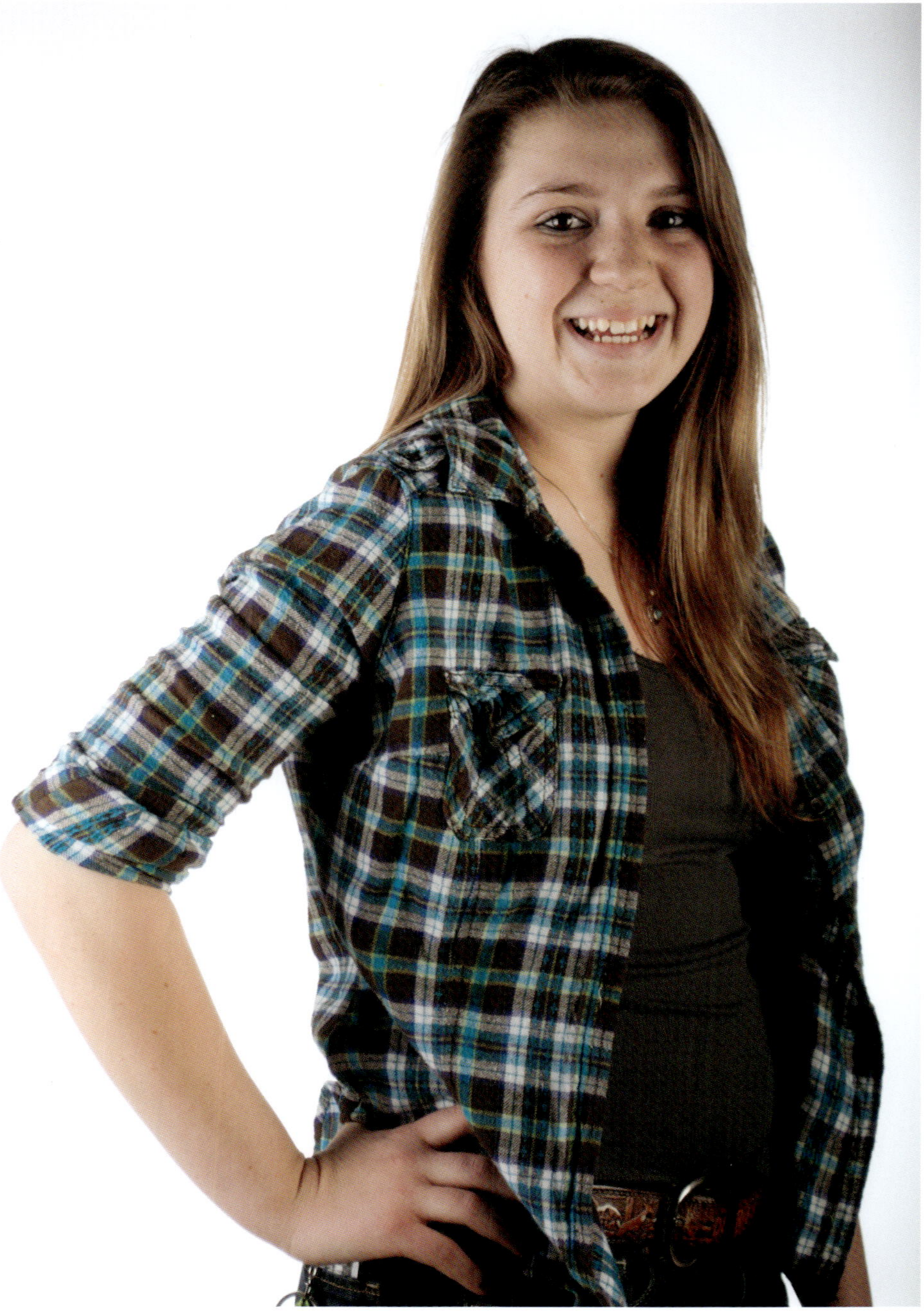

Lacey Barry
Photograph by Ron Jones

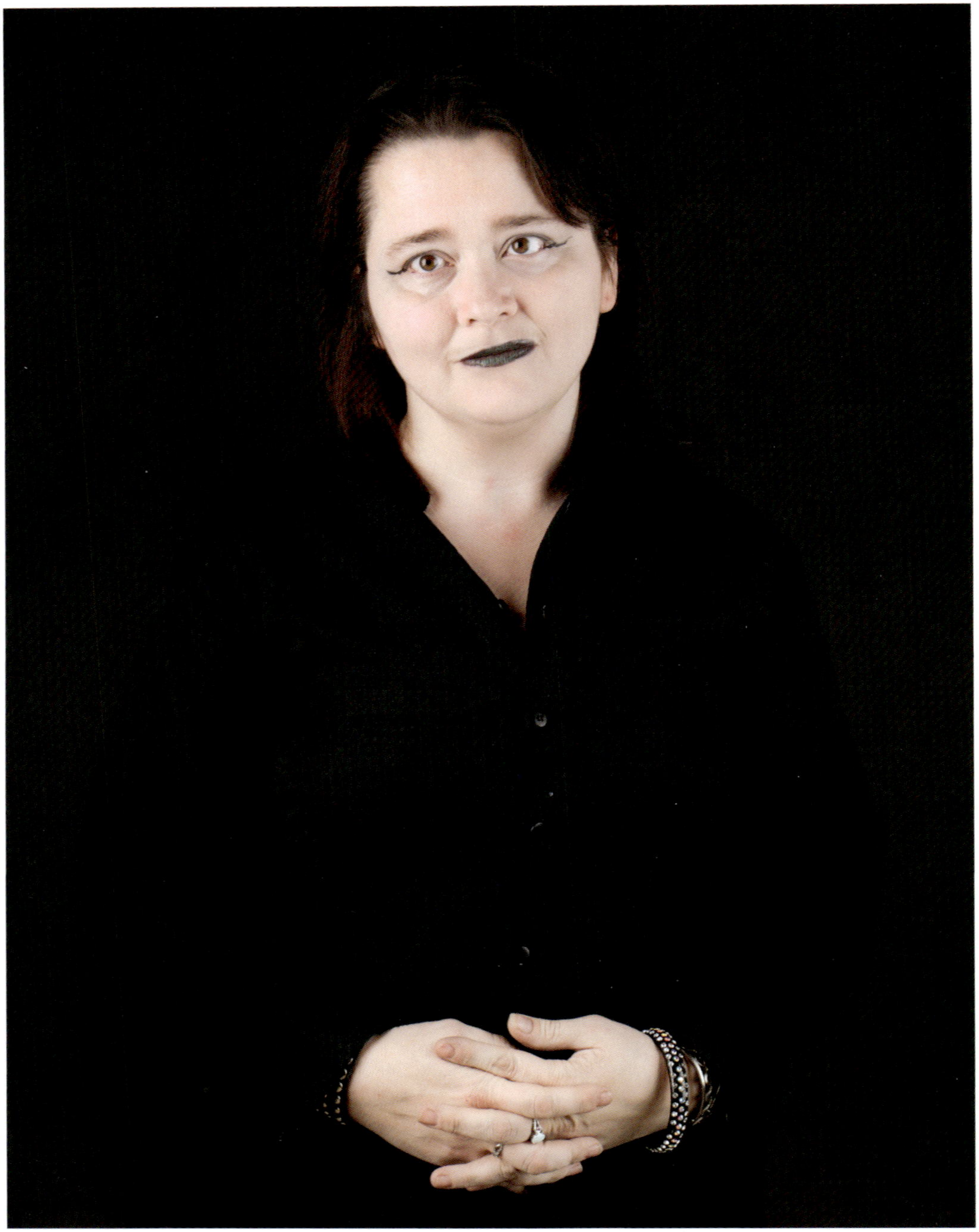

Valerie Laubenheimer
Photograph by Frederick F. Zang

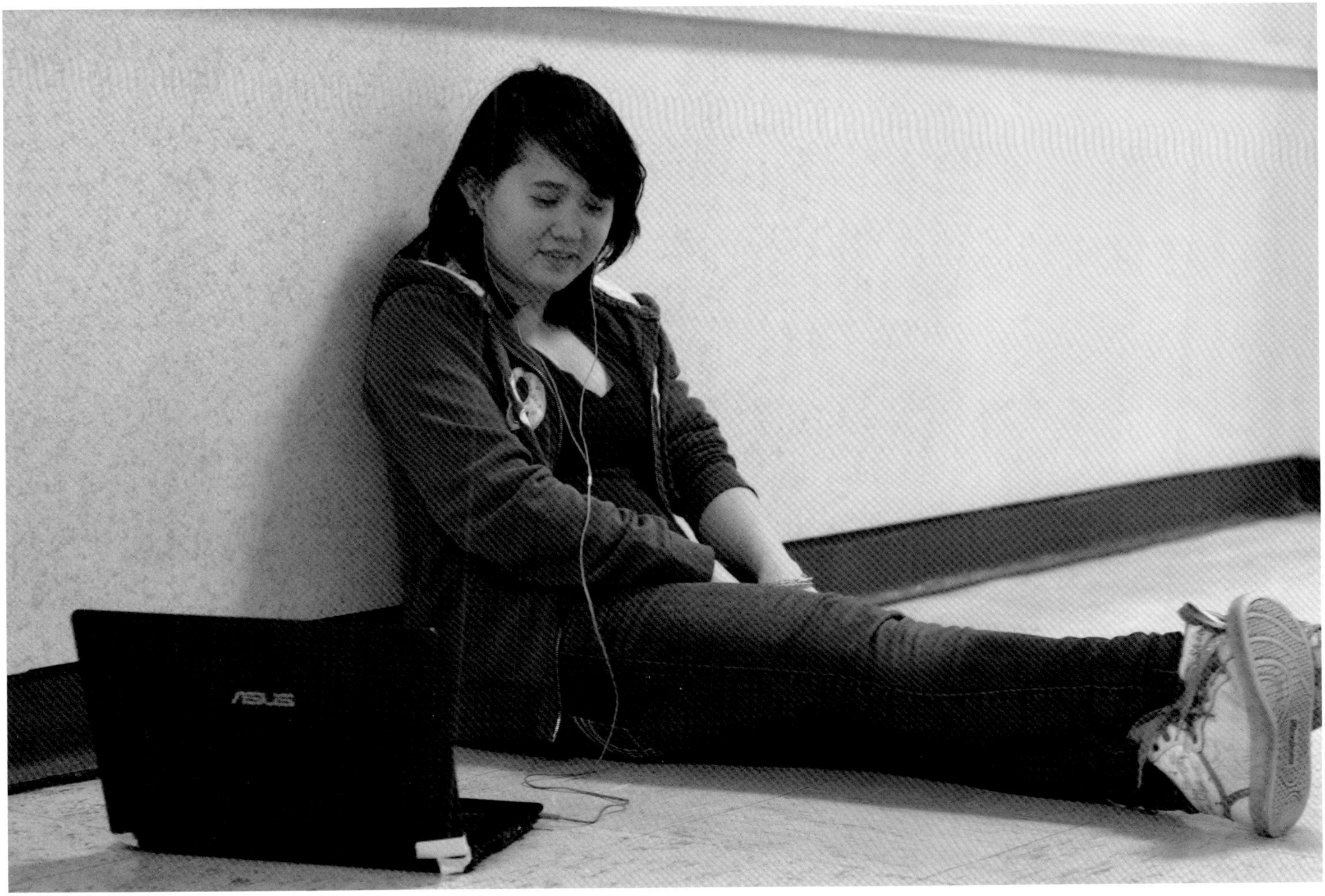

Luu Ngoc Thuy Tien
Photograph by David Lloyd

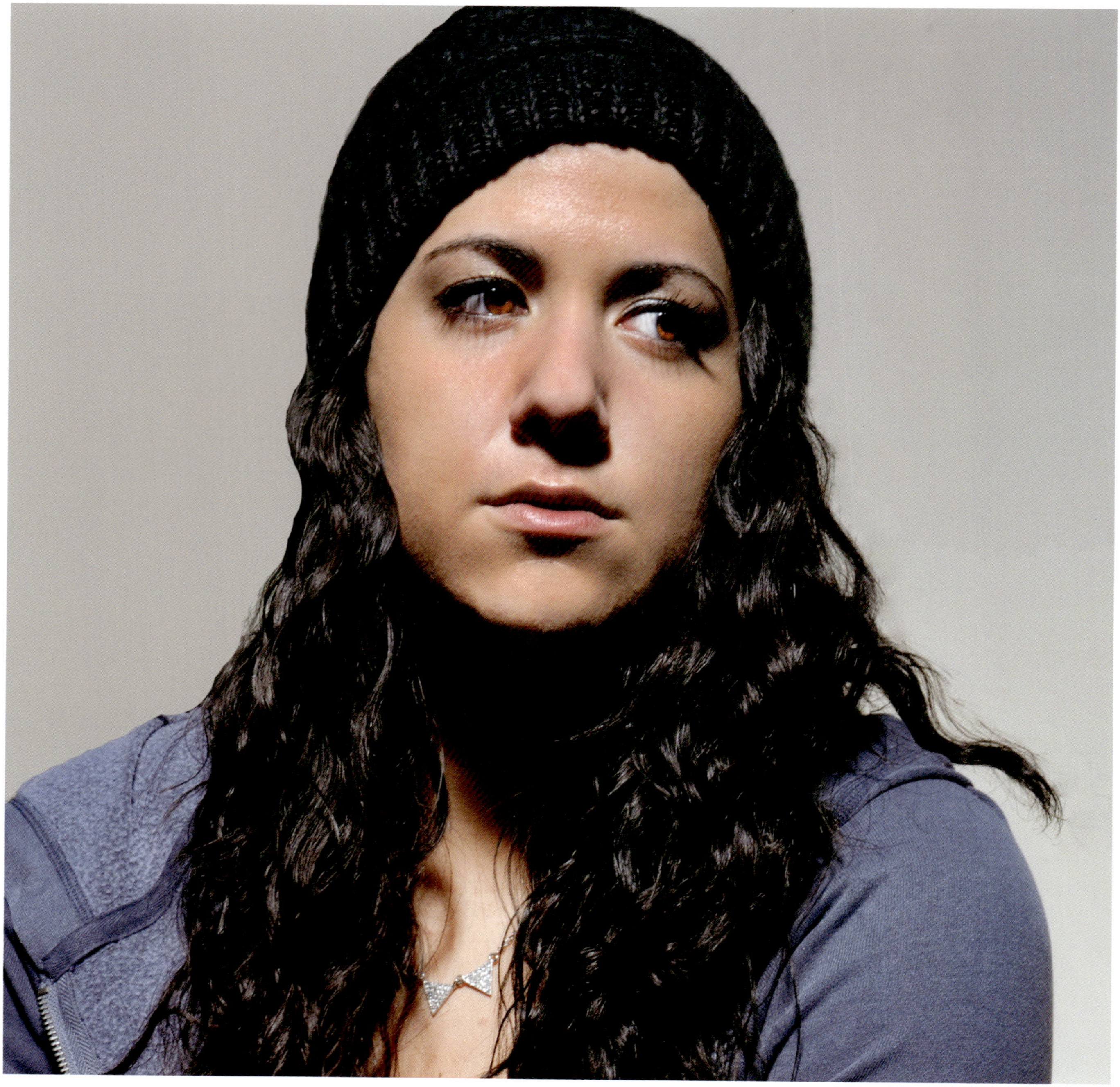

Francesca Cotrupe
Photograph by Kayla Emery

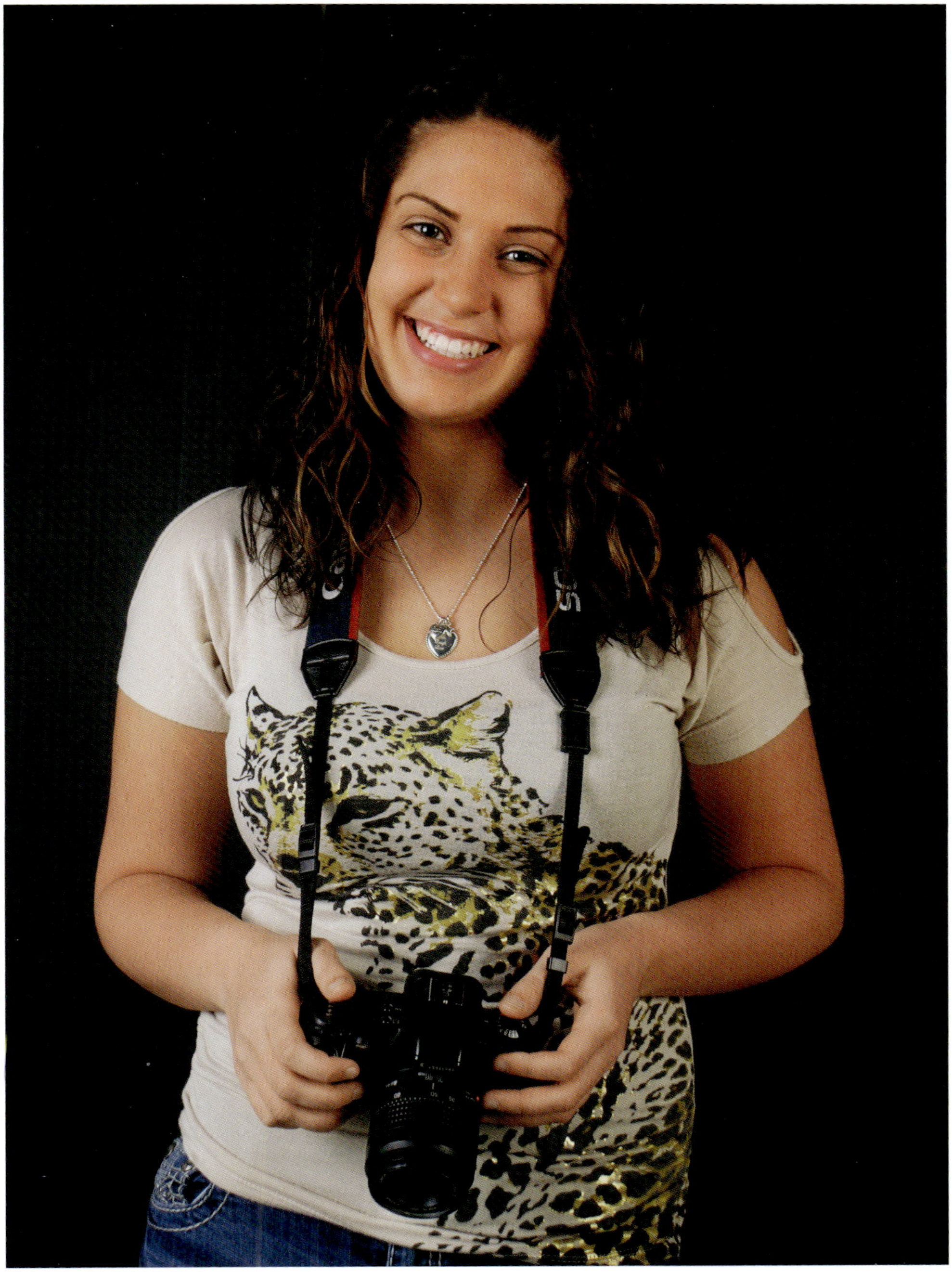

Arianna Gabriella Kousouros
Photograph by Dale Marie Romleski

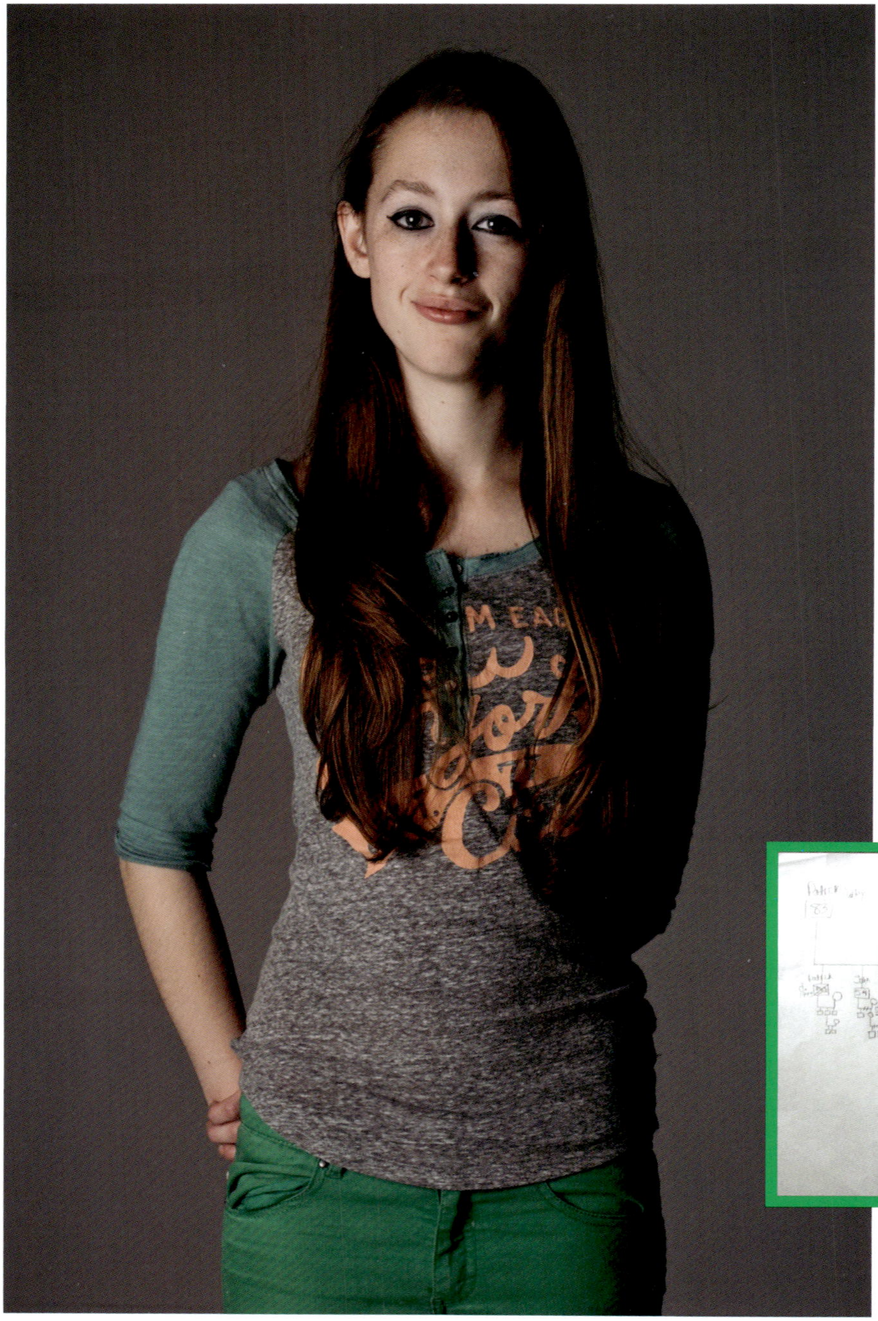

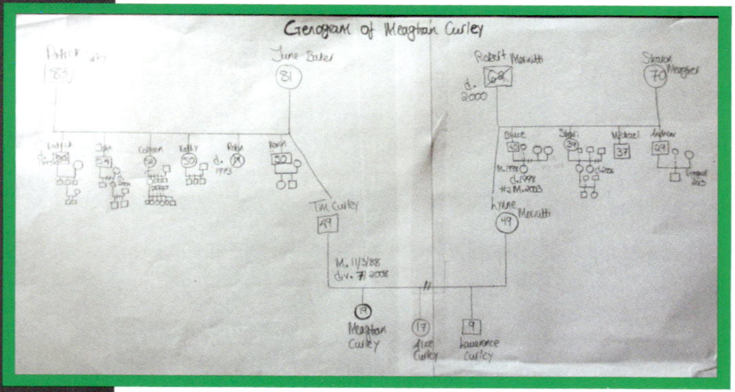

Meaghan Curley

Photograph by Frederick F. Zang

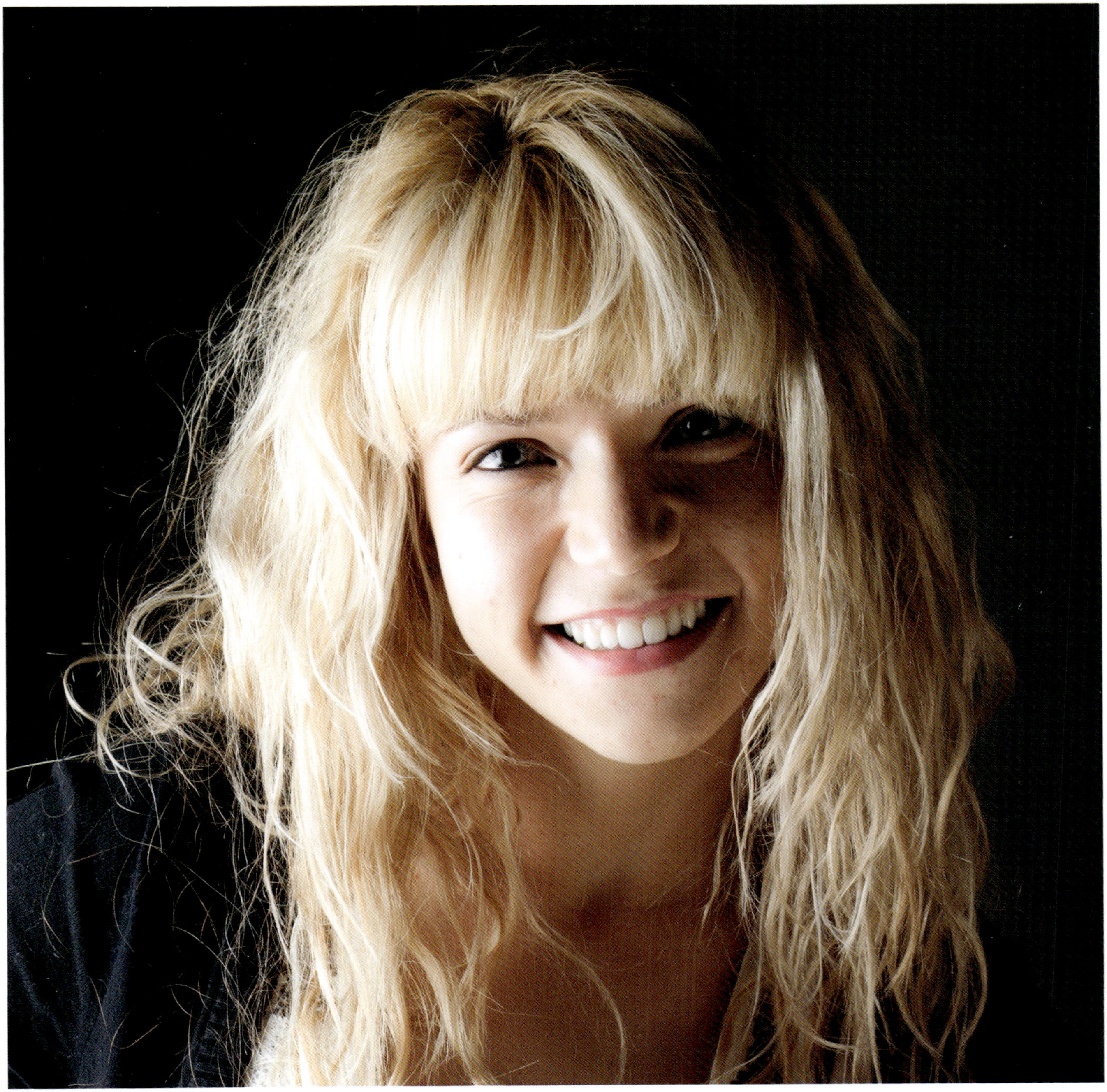

Olga Shepelevich
Photograph by Ron Jonea

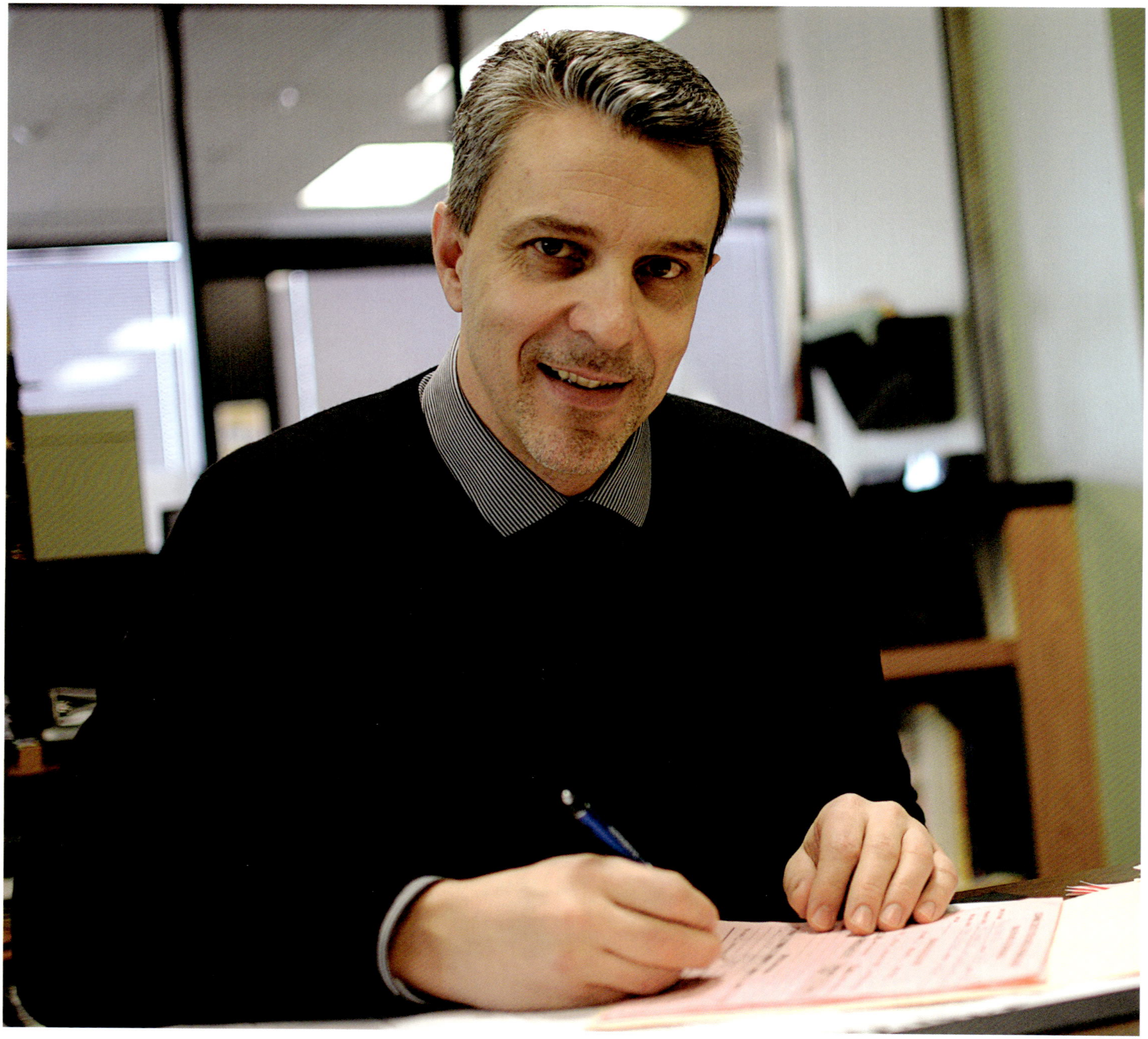

Ibrahim Rosic
Photograph by Frederick F. Zang

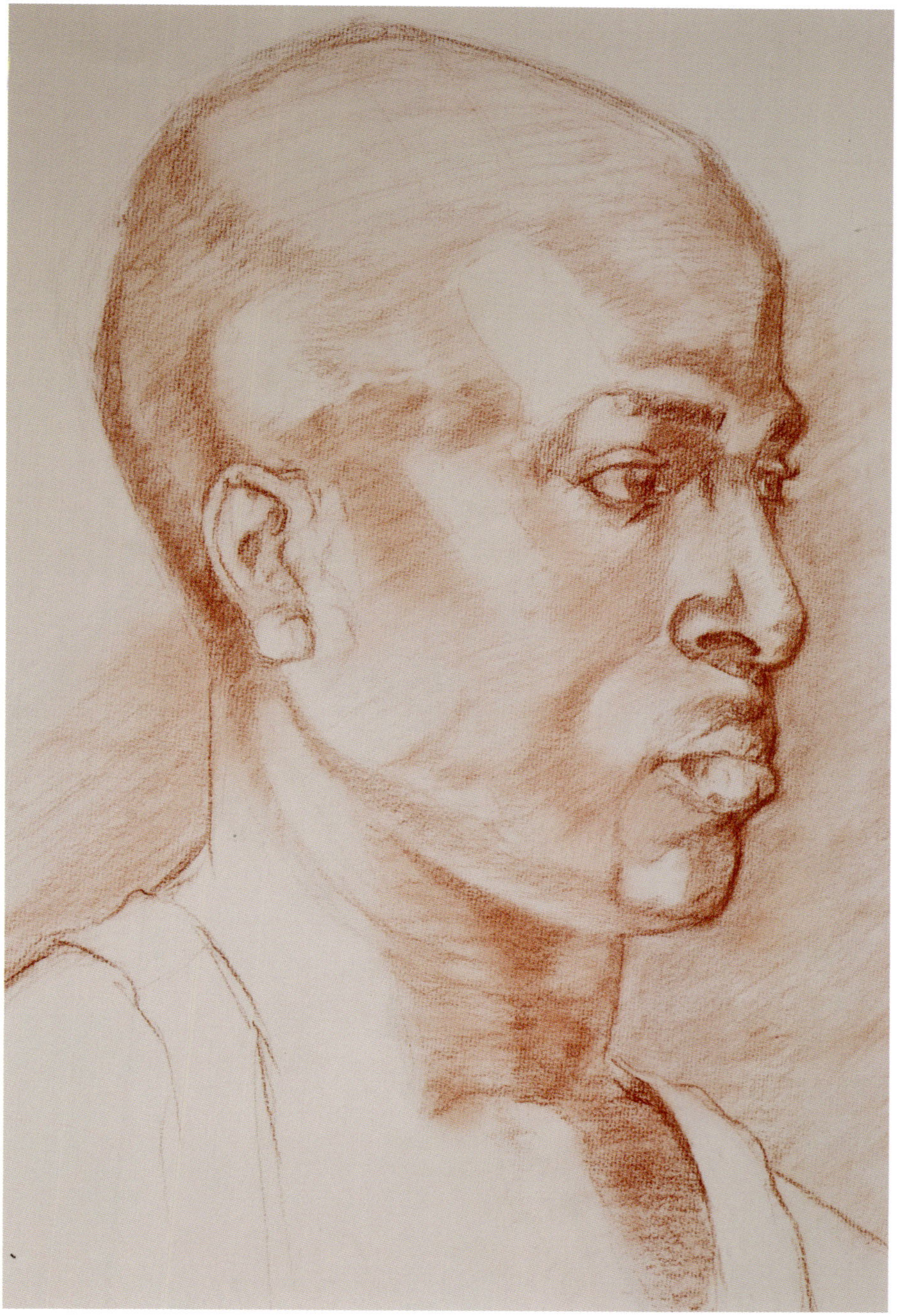

Malcolm James
Drawing by Jim Vitale

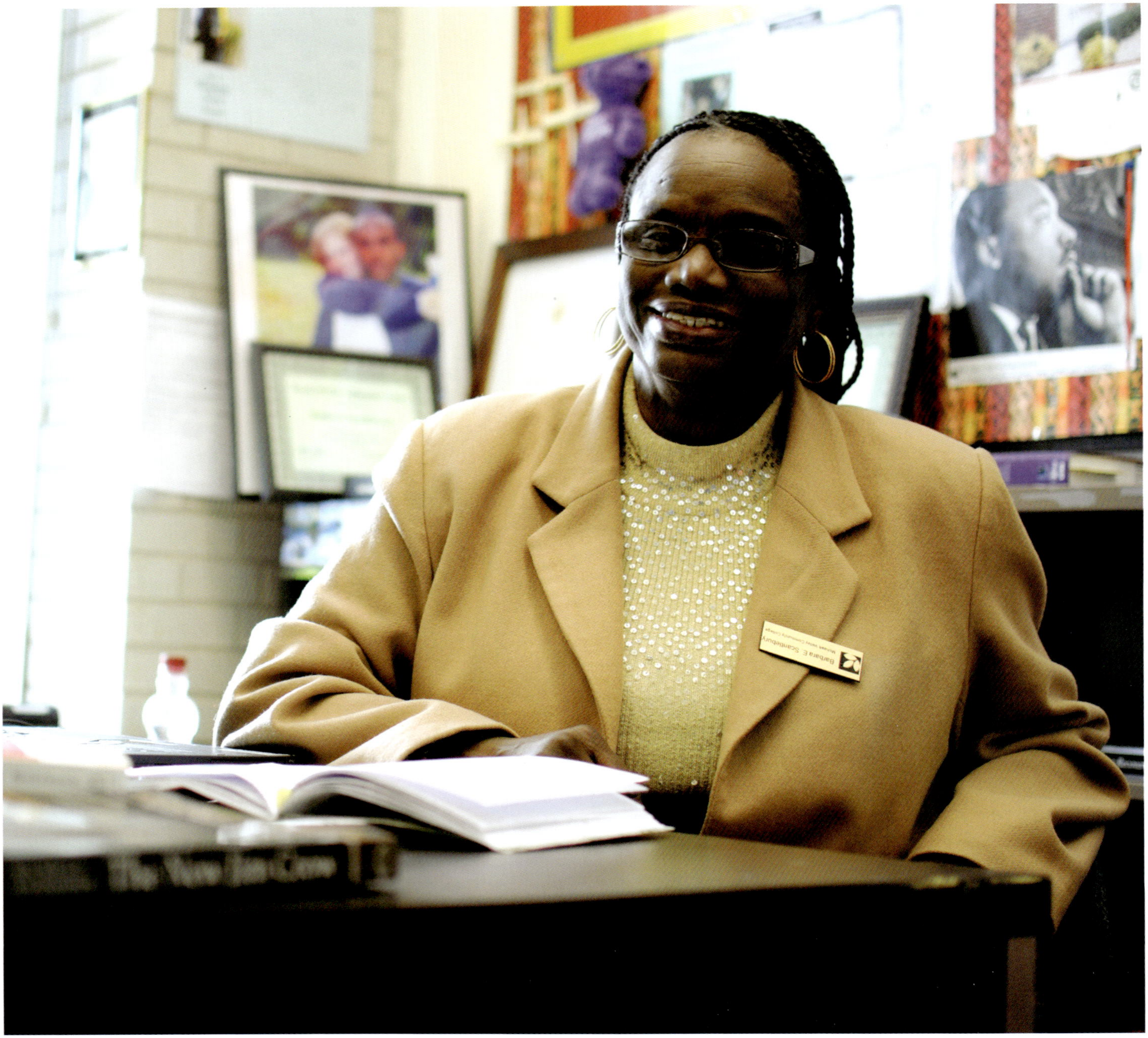

Dr. Barbara Scantlebury

Photograph by Frederick F. Zang

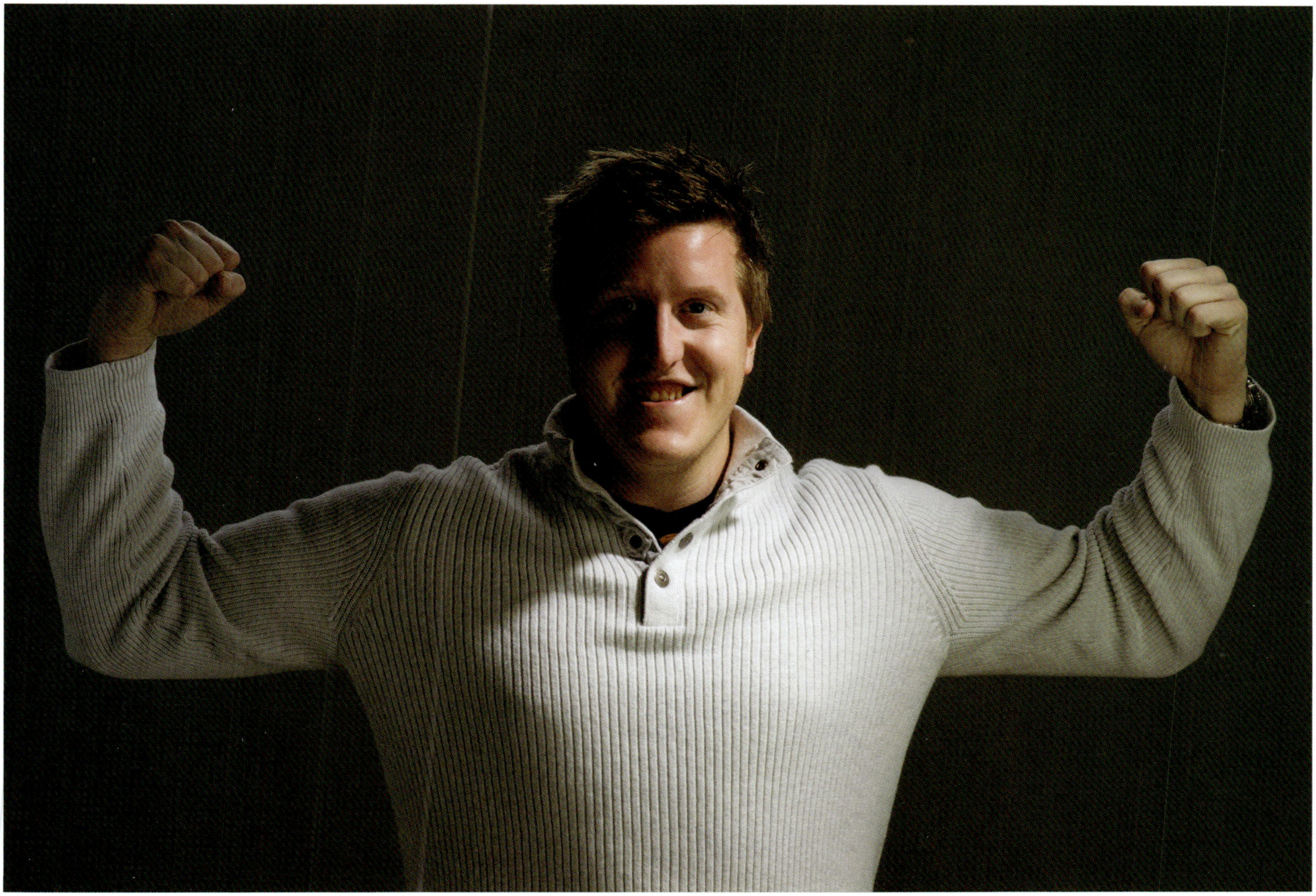

Johan Hallström
Photograph by Christopher Wilczek

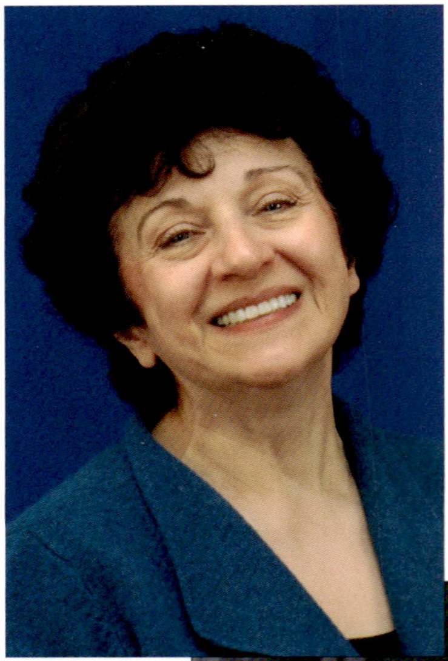

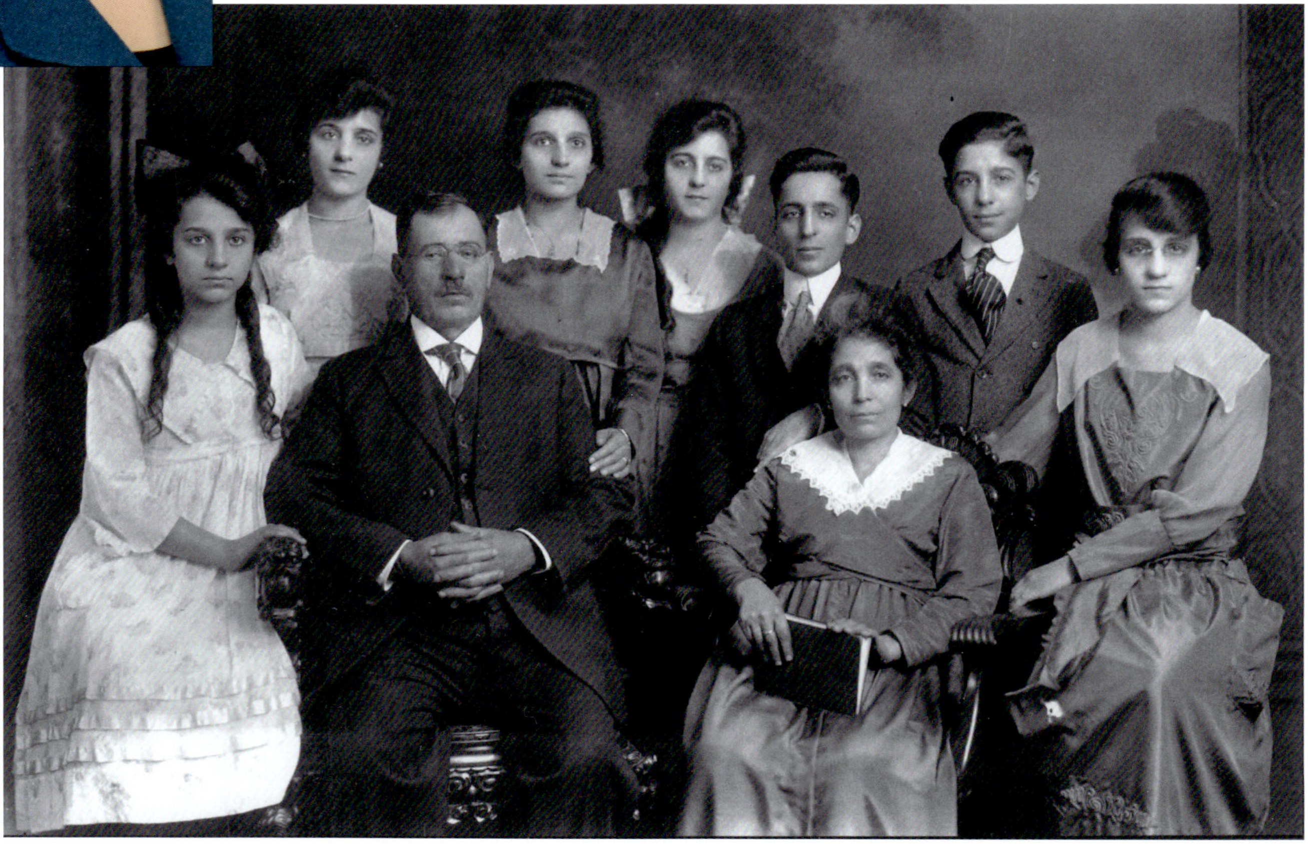

Scala Family and Maryrose Eannace

Photograph by Sharon Kane Zohne

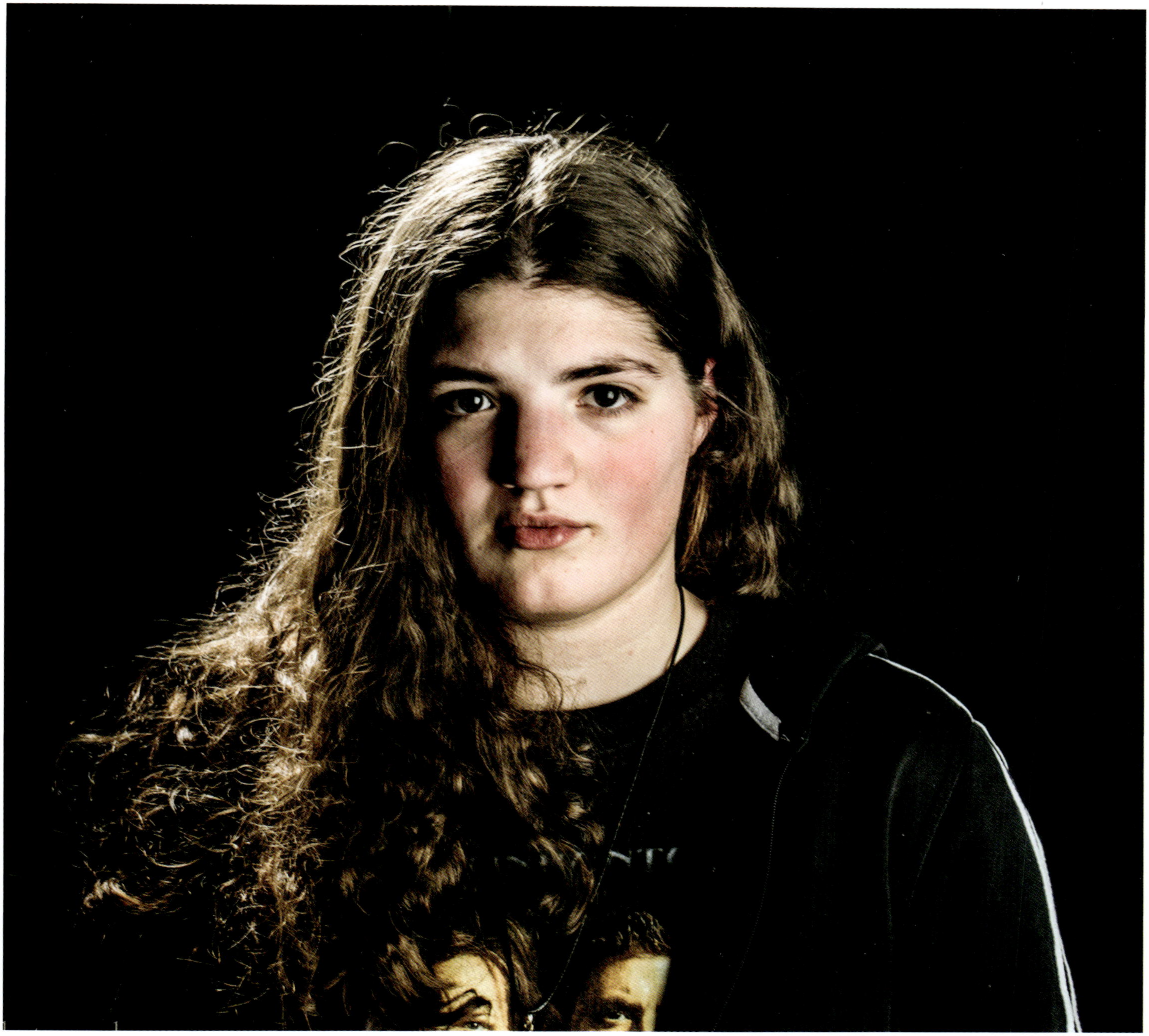

Michelle Cole
Photograph by Eden Richardson

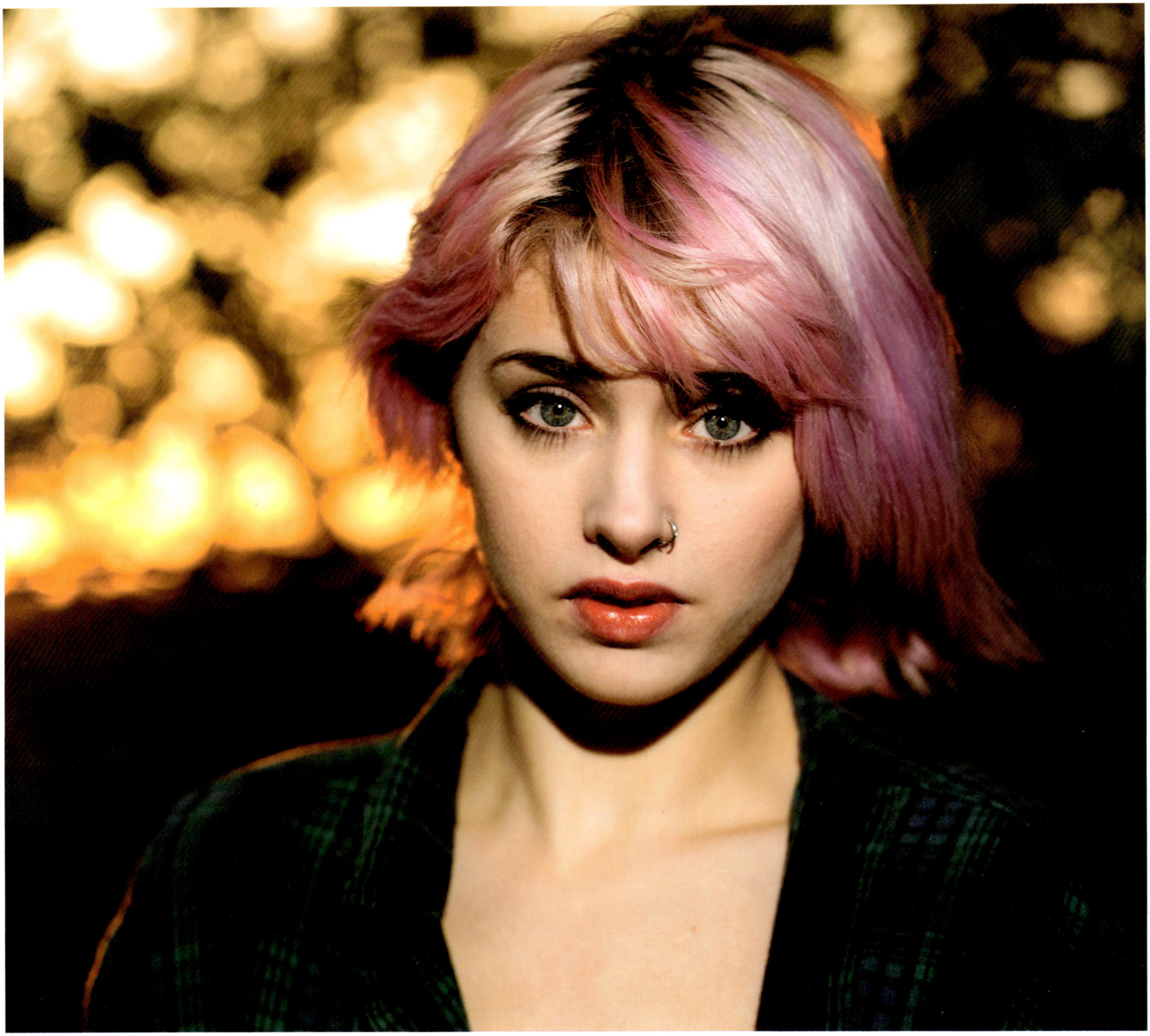

Rachel Baye
Photograph by Christian T. Stewart

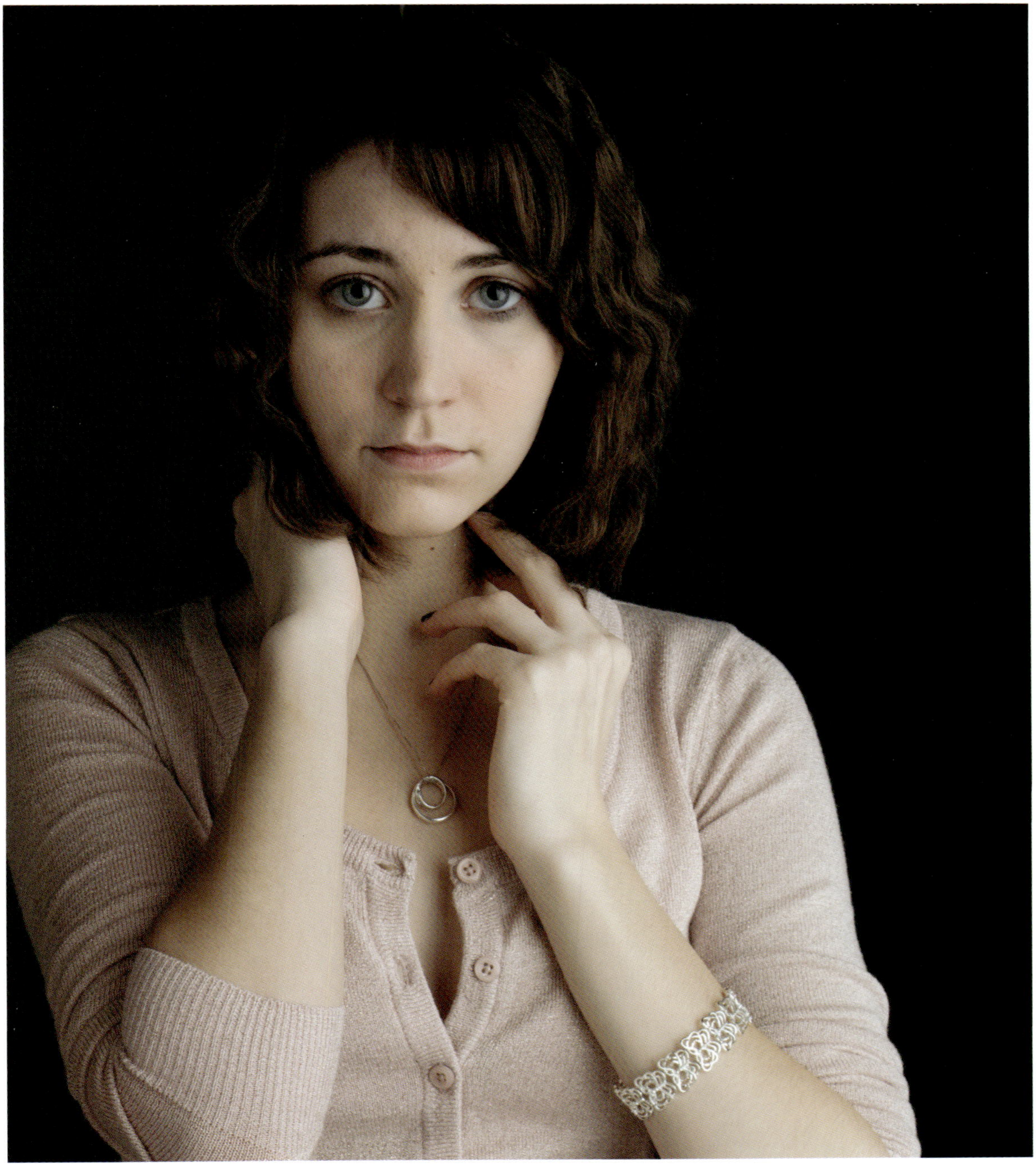

Kara Hollowell
Photograph by Stephany Vargas

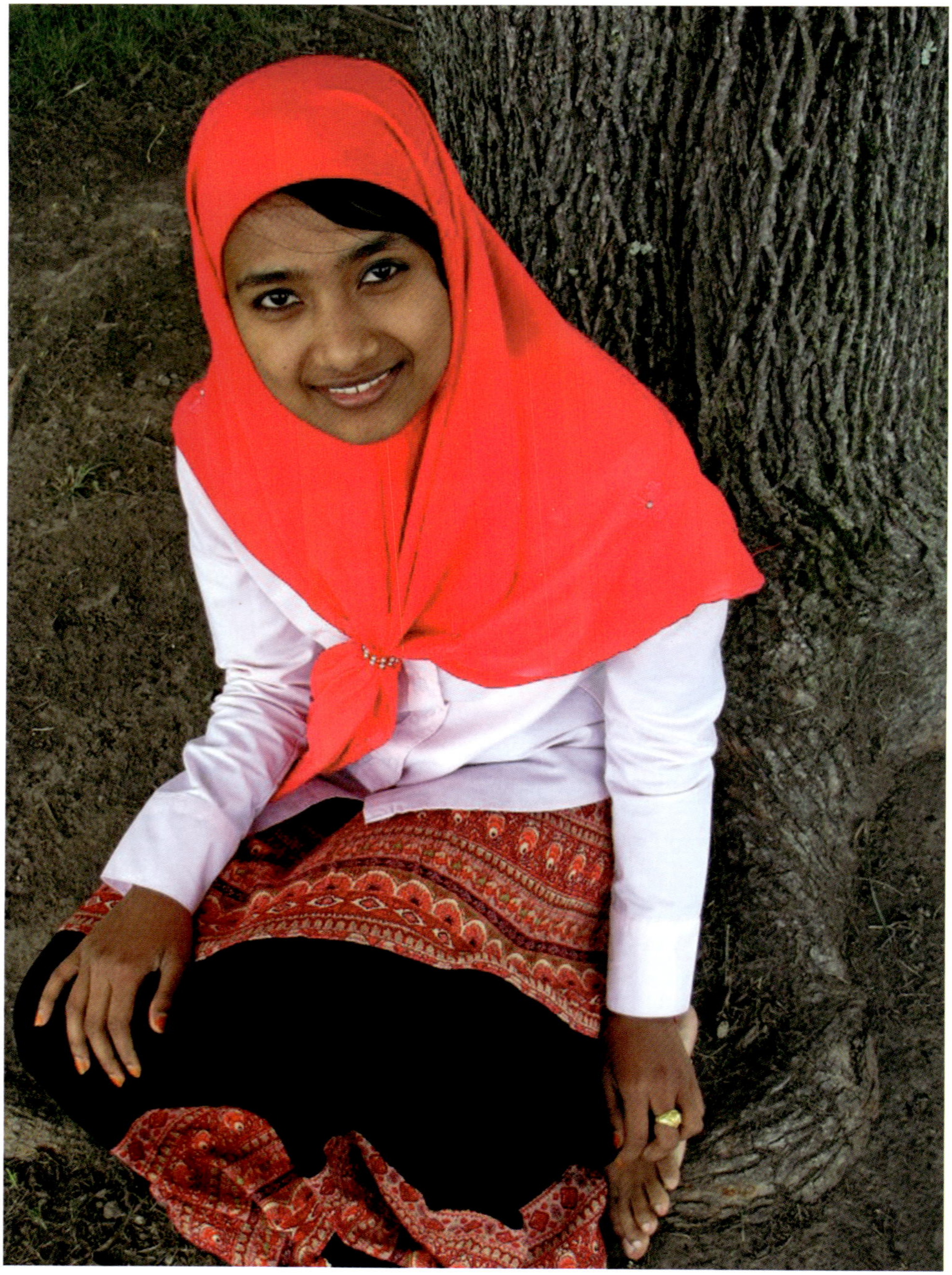

Ra Si
Photograph by De'Anna Hopkinson

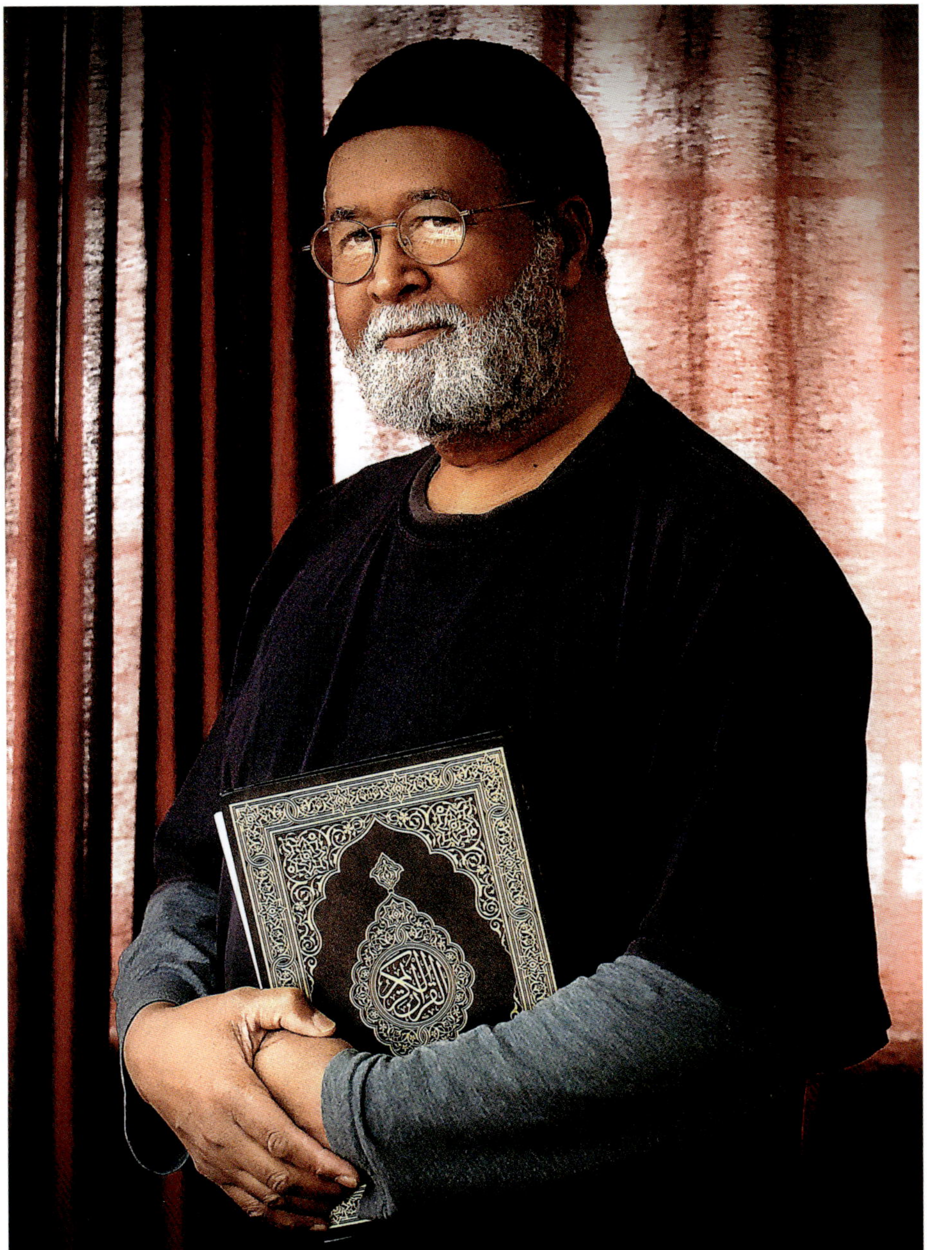

Sabur Abdul-Salaam
Photograph by Michael LaPolla

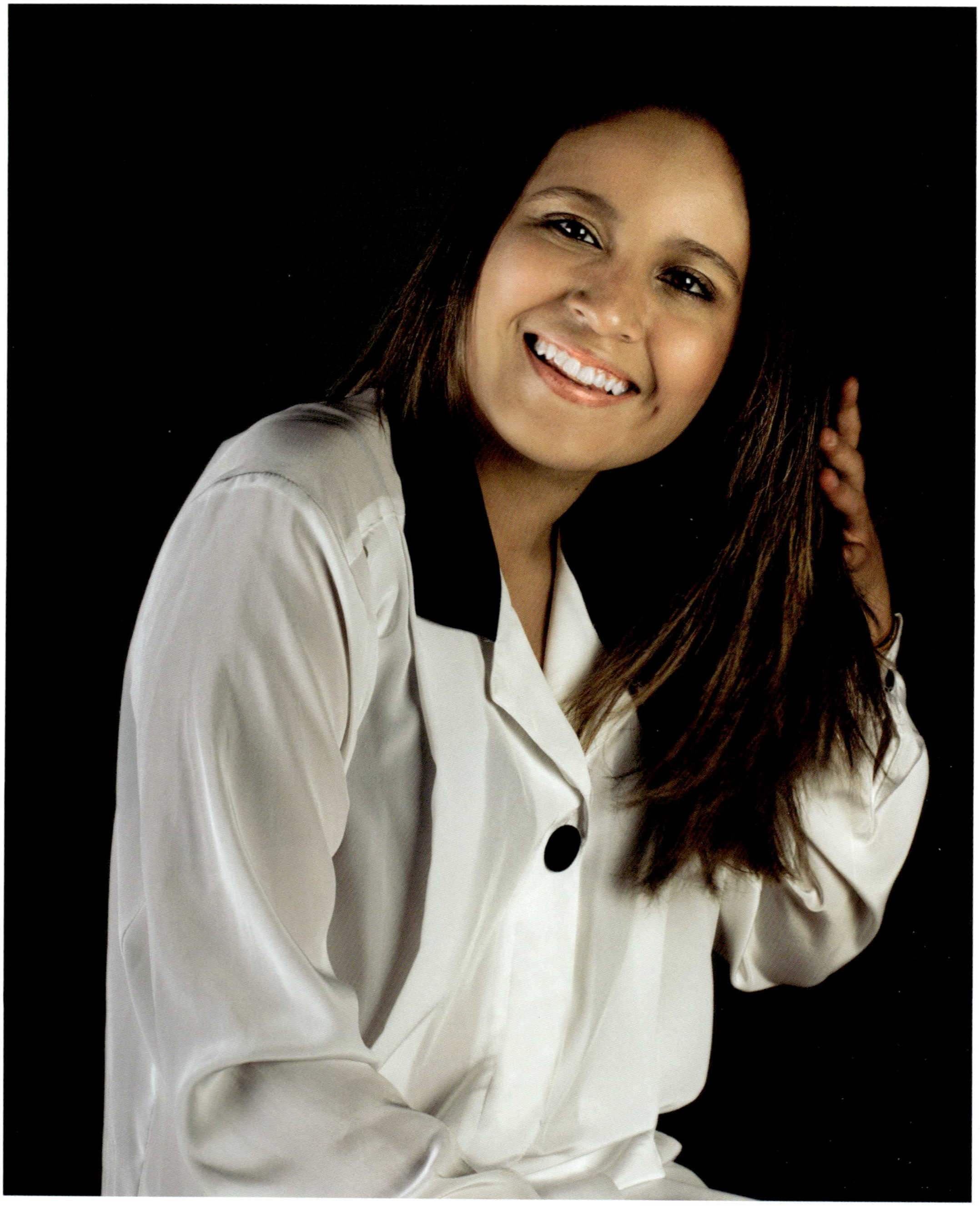

Micaela Altieri
Photograph by Jacob Dowker

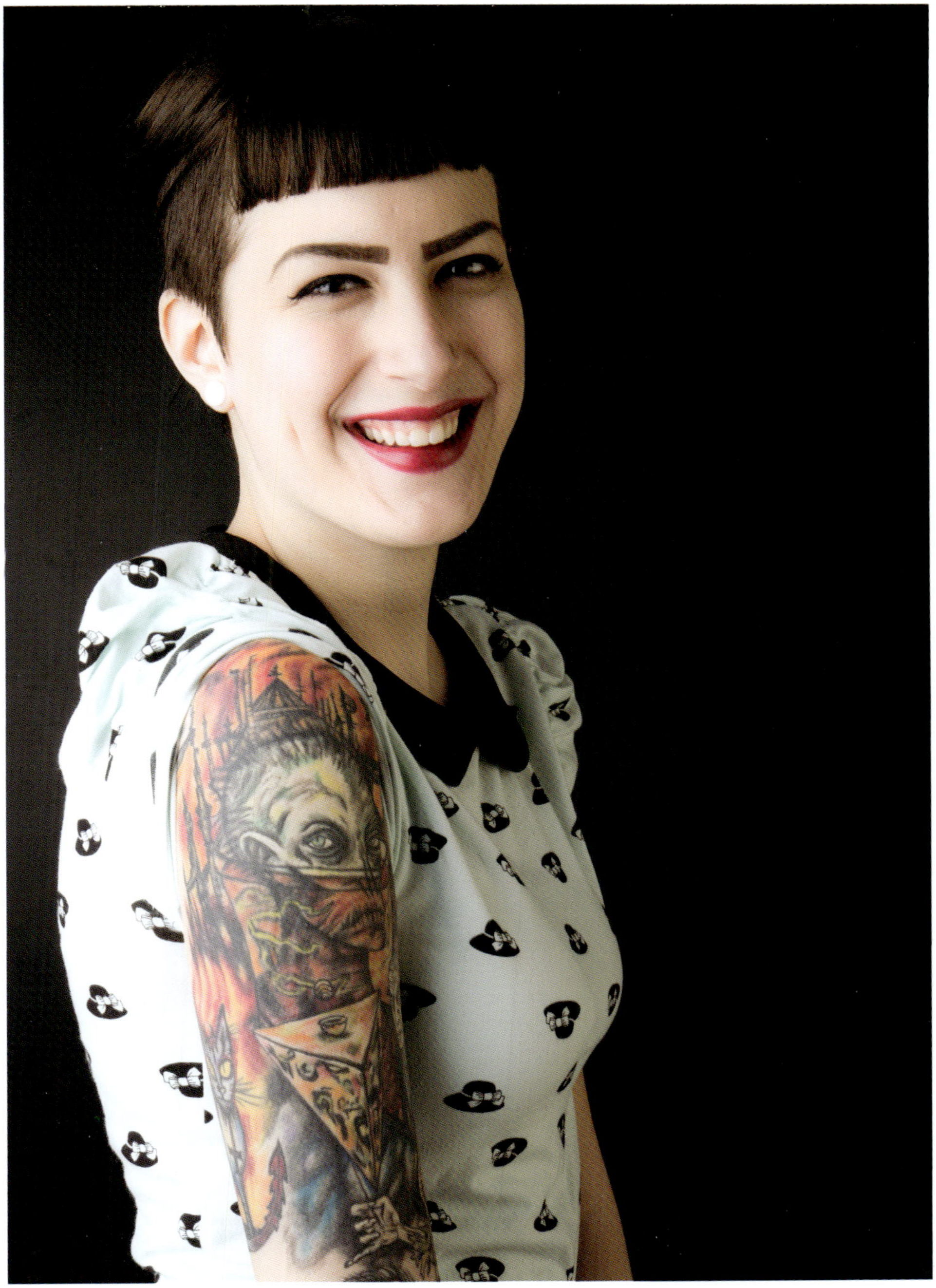

Lindsay Loson
Photograph by Anthony Zegarelli

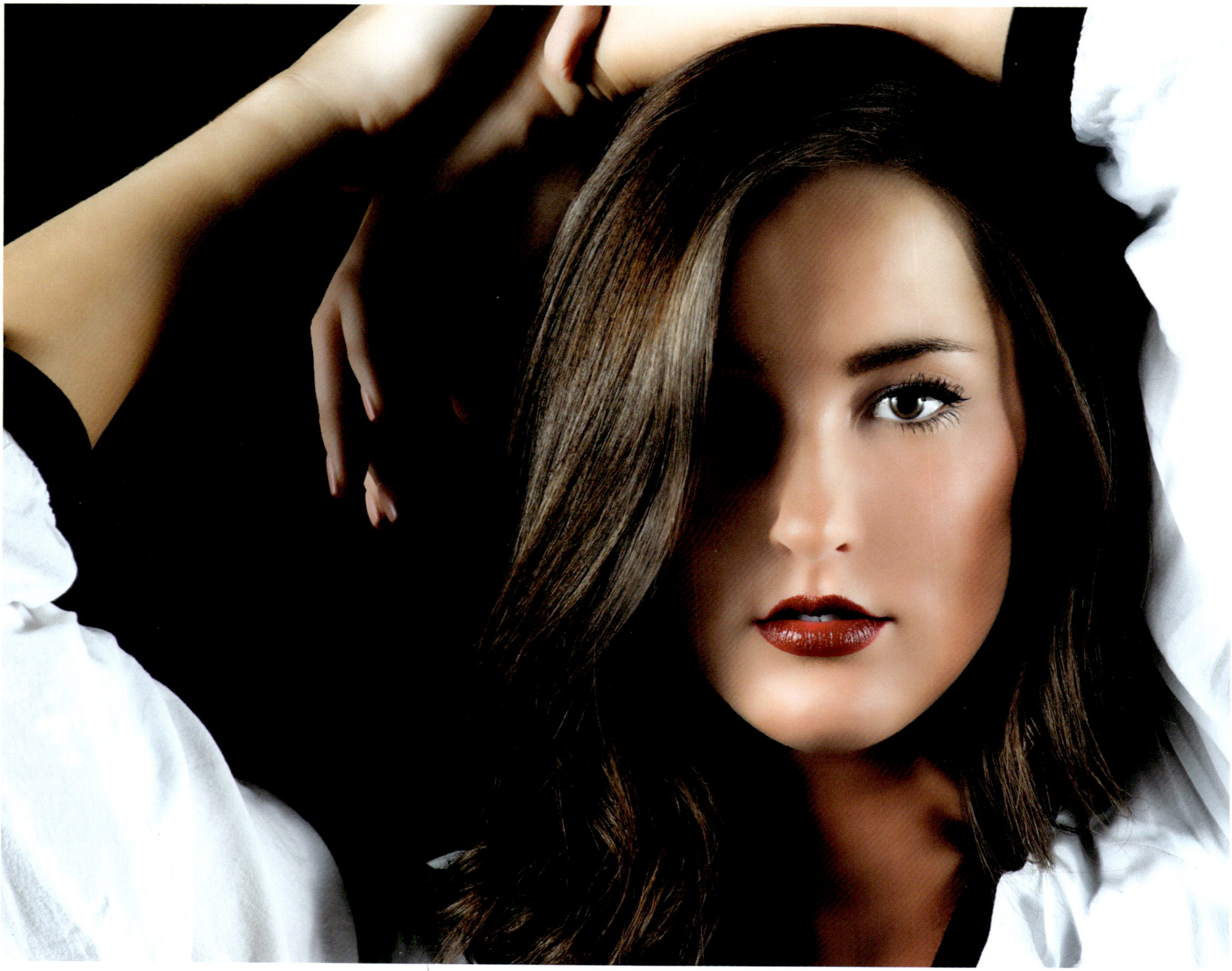

Aly Bulak
Photograph by Fred Zang & Micaela Altieri

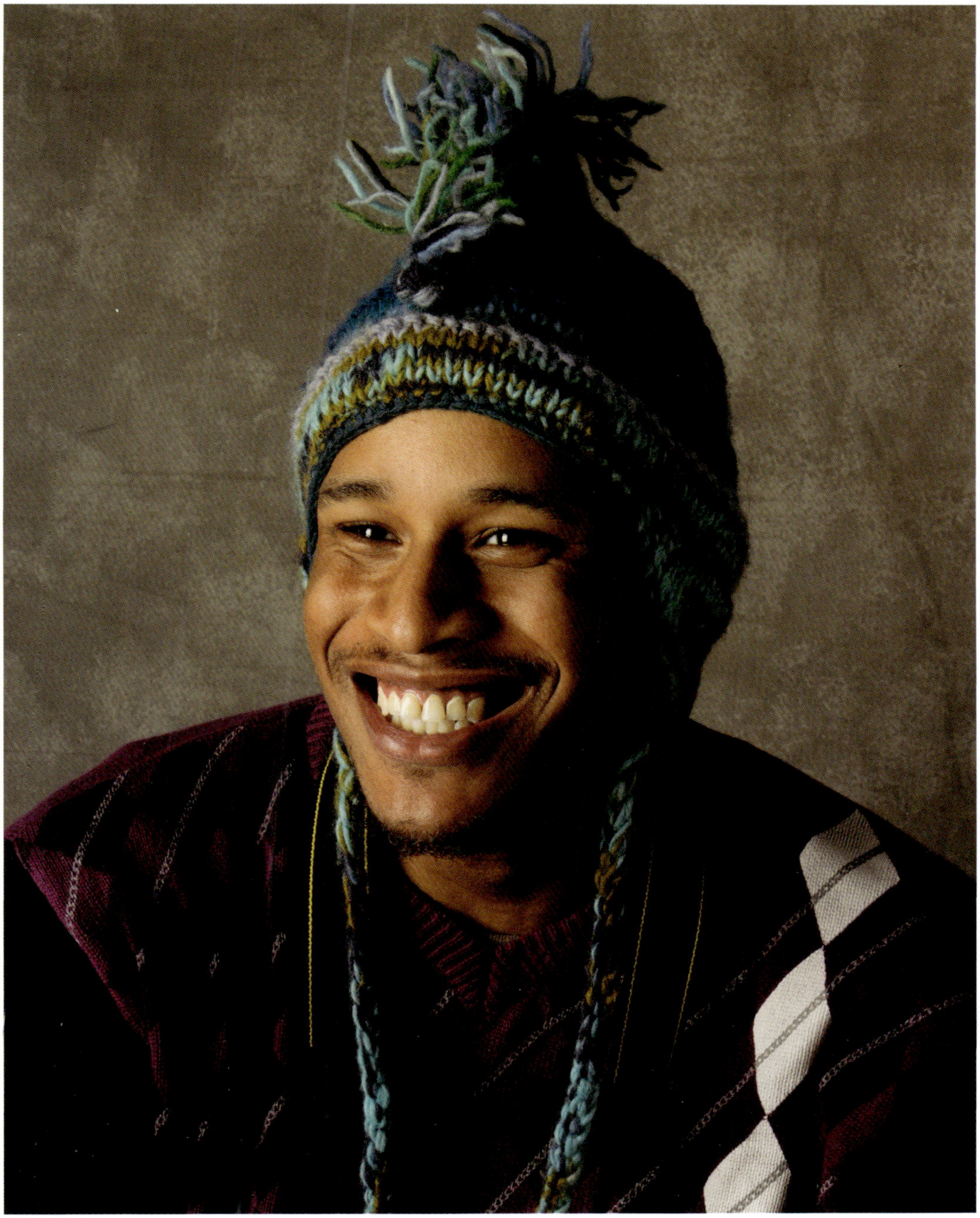

Martell J. Funney
Photograph by Valerie Laubenheimer

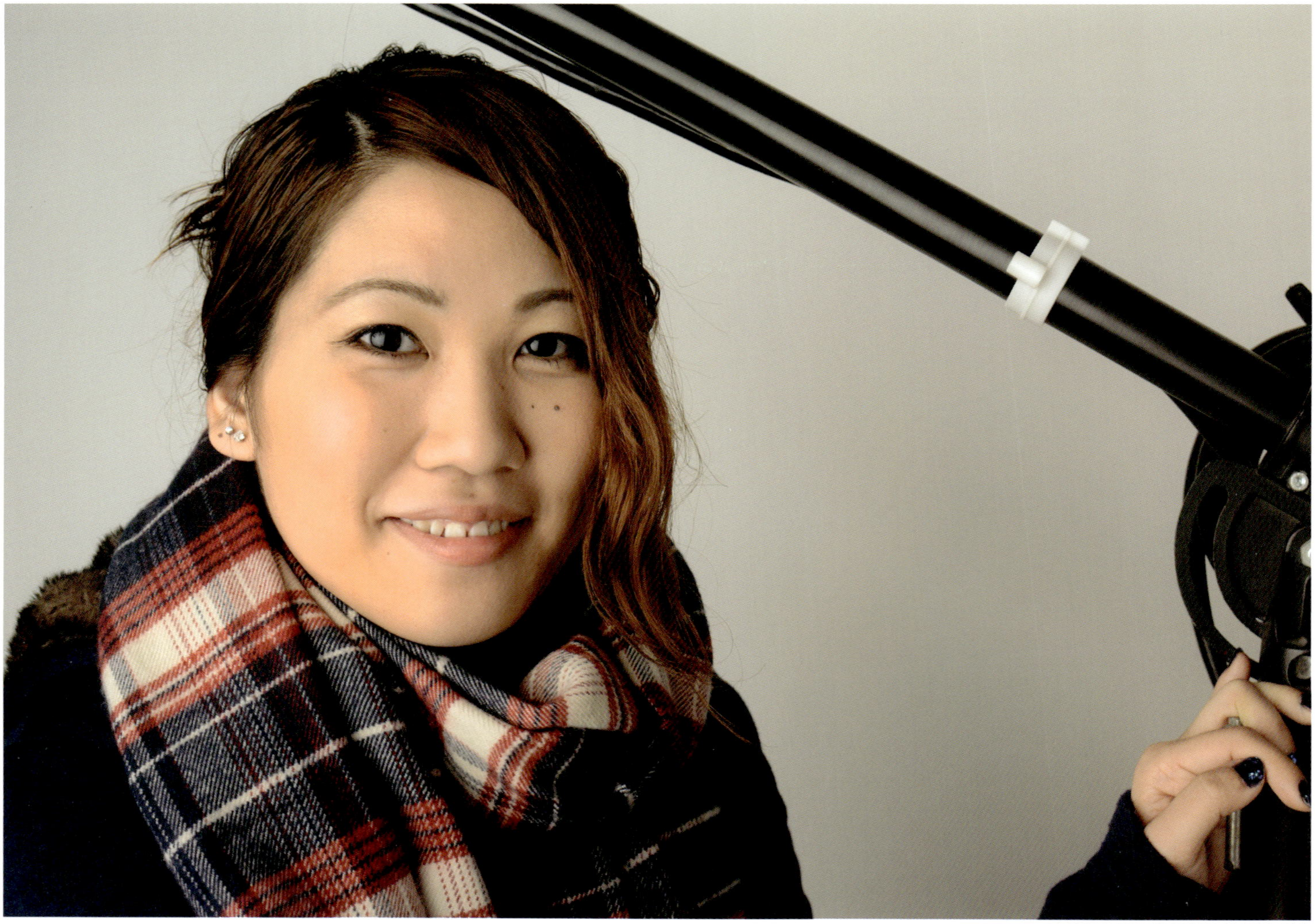

Wakana Yamada
Photograph by Joshua F. Pitcher

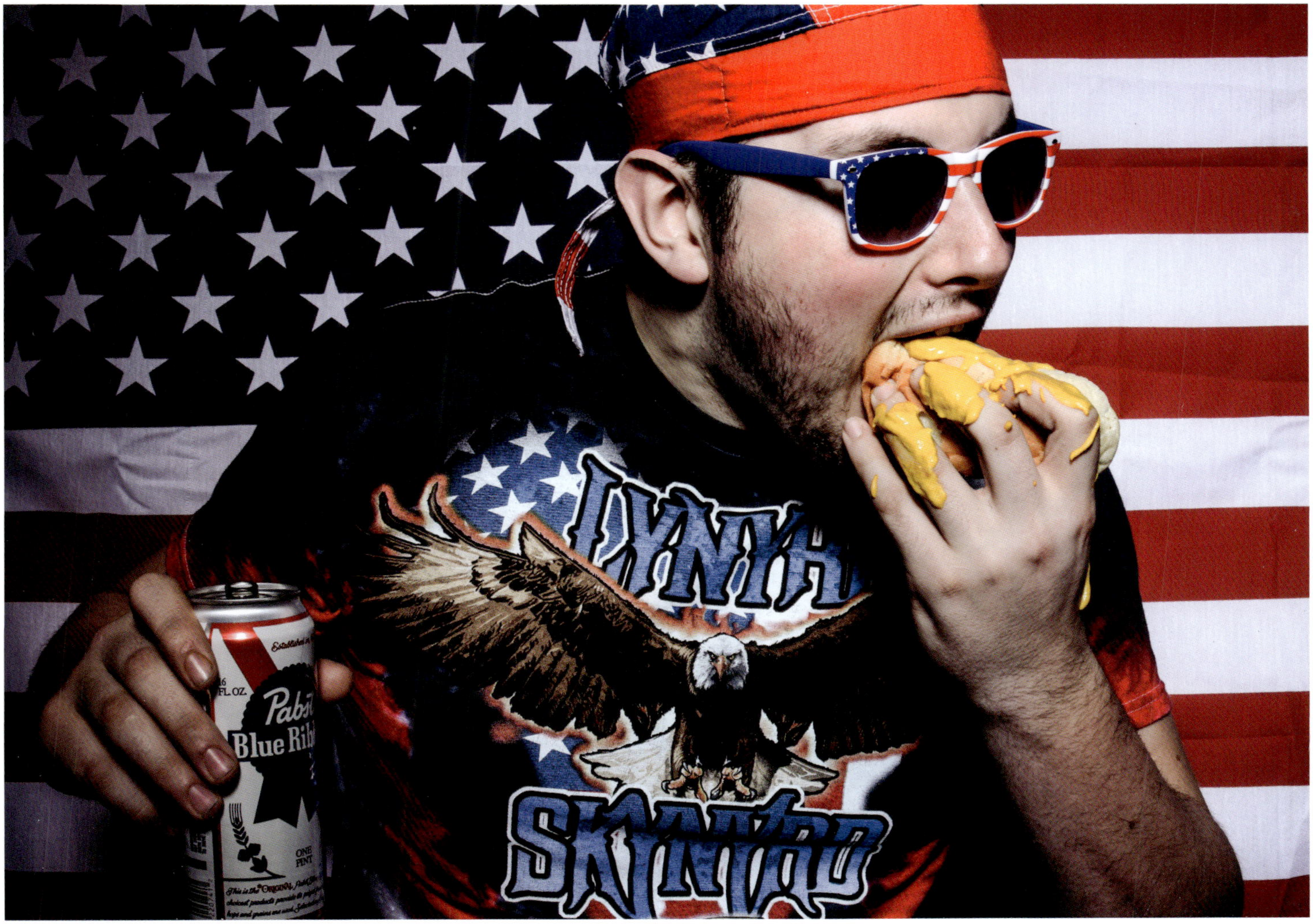

David Lloyd
Photograph by Frederick F. Zang

The People

Identity

The Artists & Photographers

The essence of all beautiful art, all great art, is gratitude.
Frederich Nietzsche